STARK'S FAMOUS

An assemblage of prominent characters
throughout our history.

Collected by The Canton Repository

STARK'S FAMOUS

An assemblage of prominent characters
throughout our history.

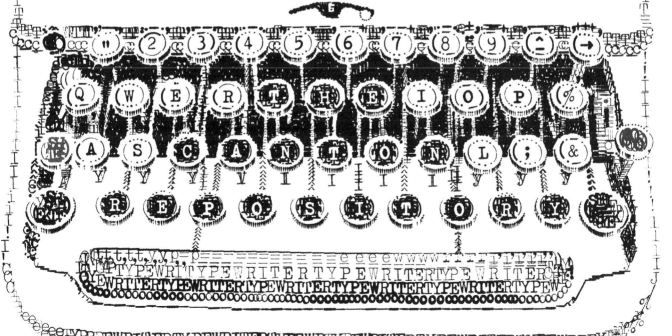

ISBN: 978-0-692-81654-7

10 9 8 7 6 5 4 3 2 1

THE CANTON REPOSITORY | GATEHOUSE OHIO MEDIA
500 MARKET AVENUE S, CANTON, OHIO 44702
(330) 580-8300 | CANTONREP.COM

JIM PORTER, PUBLISHER & CEO

MAUREEN ATER, GENERAL MANAGER

JESS BENNETT, VICE PRESIDENT, MAGAZINE DIVISION

RICH DESROSIERS, EXECUTIVE EDITOR

SCOTT BROWN, MANAGING EDITOR

LAURA KESSEL, ENGAGEMENT EDITOR

DAVE MANLEY, VISUAL CONTENT EDITOR

KELSEY REINHART, MAGAZINE DIVISION EDITOR

COVER DESIGN: JESS BENNETT

BOOK DESIGN: MURPHY REDMOND & KELSEY REINHART

STARK'S FAMOUS PROFILES COMPILED BY CANTON REPOSITORY STAFF

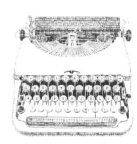

CONTENTS

INTRODUCTION

Acclaimed. Distinguished. Illustrious. Beloved.

Famous.

In our long history of service to Stark County and its residents, we have been reminded time and again about the area's rich history and the importance of its people, people who go on to shape our area, our state and our country.

In 2016, we took a look back through the pages of our history to find Stark County's most "famous"-folks from all walks of life, serving in politics, sports, entertainment, public service, education and medicine. Folks who have connections to Stark County and who have made Stark County-and beyond-great.

Each day in 2016, we revealed a new profile of Stark's Famous, selected by our editorial team with input from readers. We now offer to you an assemblage of all 366 of Stark's Famous, along with a few bonus profiles, in one collection in the hopes that it will stand as a testament to the aptitude and influence of Stark County and her people.

This book is dedicated to those who comprise Stark's Famous, in the hopes that they will pave the way for many more pages of profiles to come in the future.

-The Canton Repository staff

S T A R K ' S
F A M O U S

STARK'S FAMOUS

A year's worth of Stark County's most noteworthy and notable people,
as seen in the 2016 daily pages of The Canton Repository.

WILLIAM McKINLEY

"That's all a man can hope for during his lifetime — to set an example — and when he is dead, to be an inspiration for history."

ABOUT
- Born Jan. 29, 1843, in Niles.
- Died Sept. 14, 1901, in Buffalo, New York.
- 25th president of the United States, serving 1897-1901.
- Assassinated six months into second term.
- 39th governor of Ohio, serving from 1892-96.
- Elected to Congress in 1876, serving from 1877-91.
- Served in Union Army in Civil War.

STARK CONNECTION
- After the war, settled in Canton, where he practiced law and married Ida Saxton.
- Attended Allegheny College.
- Attended classes at Albany College Law School.

ALAN PAGE

"The way to be successful is through preparation. It doesn't just happen. You don't wake up one day and discover you're a lawyer any more than you wake up as a pro football player. It takes time."

ABOUT
- Born Alan Cedric Page on Aug. 7, 1945.
- First black justice on Minnesota Supreme Court.
- Educated at University of Minnesota Law School.
- Enshrined in Pro Football Hall of Fame in 1988.
- NFL Rookie of the Year, MVP, 9-time Pro Bowl selection.
- NFL defensive lineman for 16 years for Minnesota Vikings and Chicago Bears.
- Played football for and graduated from Notre Dame.

STARK CONNECTION
- Graduated from Central Catholic High School in 1963.
- Part of construction crew helping to build Football Hall of Fame.

LILLIAN GISH

"I've never been in style, so I can never go out of style."

ABOUT
- Born Oct. 14, 1893, in Springfield.
- Died Feb. 27, 1993, in New York City.
- Silent-film star known as "The First Lady of American Cinema."
- Had leading roles in D.W. Griffith's silent classics "Birth of a Nation" (1915) and "Intolerance" (1916).
- Academy Award nominee in 1946 for "A Duel in the Sun."
- Received a lifetime achievement award in 1984 from the American Film Institute.

STARK CONNECTION
- Summered as a girl with her sister Dorothy at their aunt's house at 315 Fourth St. NE in Massillon.
- Spoke in 1951 at the completion of Massillon's flood control project.
- In 1984, spoke at St. Timothy's Episcopal Church.

CORNELIUS AULTMAN

"Aultman was a Stark County farm boy who became one of America's most successful and respected businessmen during the Civil War Era."

— HISTORIAN RICHARD HALDI

ABOUT
- Born March 10, 1827, near Canton.
- Died Dec. 26, 1884, at home in Canton.
- Leading manufacturer of farm equipment.
- Sold reapers and threshers and known for the Buckeye Mower.
- Assets at his death estimated at nearly $2 million.
- Well-known as a philanthropist.
- Due to donations made by his family following his death, Aultman Hospital named after him.

STARK CONNECTION
- Stark County native.
- Most of his businesses were based locally.

MOTHER ANGELICA

"A soul that trusts God is invincible."

ABOUT
- Rita Antoinette Rizzo was born April 20, 1923.
- Known as the "Fishing Lure Nun" for making and selling them as a fundraiser
- Established Our Lady of the Angels Monastery in Alabama in the 1960s.
- Founded the Eternal Word Television Network in the 1980s.
- Was host of the "Mother Angelica Live" talk show from 1981 to 2001.

STARK CONNECTION
- Canton native who went to McKinley High School.
- Was a cloistered nun at Sancta Clara Monastery in the 1950s.

RENEE POWELL

"I know I have been referred to as a trailblazer in golf, but really, this is what I have done all my life. I didn't have to play the piano three hours a day growing up. Instead, I played golf."

ABOUT
- Born May 4, 1946.
- Retired LPGA professional golfer.
- Started golfing at age 3; began competitive career at 12.
- In 2000, began the LPGA Girls Golf Club in East Canton.
- Among the first seven women to be granted membership in the Royal and Ancient Golf Club of St. Andrews Links, considered to be the home of golf.

STARK CONNECTION
- Head professional at her family's Clearview Golf Club in Osnaburg Township.
- Graduated from Central Catholic High School in 1964.

14

WILLIAM R. DAY

"For a quarter of a century he was one of the most lovable and most helpful men in public life, revered by all who knew him. We feel a personal loss at his passing."

— TELEGRAM FROM PRESIDENT WARREN G. HARDING

ABOUT
- Born April 17, 1849, in Ravenna.
- Died July 9, 1923 on Mackinac Island, Michigan.
- Associate justice of U.S. Supreme Court for almost 20 years.
- Friend and adviser to William McKinley.
- Secretary of State during the Spanish-American War.
- Sided with the government in anti-trust cases against Standard Oil, American Tobacco, Union Pacific and Southern Pacific.

STARK CONNECTION
- Settled in Canton in 1872.
- Founded law firm that became Day Ketterer.

STANLEY MACOMBER

"Even though he was a very serious engineer and a businessman, he also was a grandfather. When we'd go to visit, he'd always have lemon drops. He delighted in that. My grandfather was known for little kindness that he never crowed about."

— RICHARD MACOMBER, GRANDSON

ABOUT
- Born Nov. 26, 1887 in Iowa, died May 15, 1967 in Canton.
- In 1919, took a job with National Pressed Steel of Massillon, where he developed ideas for the open web joist floor system.
- Filed for a patent in 1923. The system is a "freeway for pipes, conduits, and ductwork," according to the National Inventors Hall of Fame and still is used to this day — take a look at the ceiling of stores, such as Lowe's or Home Depot.
- Inducted into the National Inventors Hall of Fame in 2011.

STARK CONNECTION
- Born in Iowa but moved to Canton in 1915.
- Created Massillon Steel Joist Company and Macomber Inc.

AUGUSTUS D. JUILLIARD

"A stalwart, resolute figure in the worlds of finance and business for nearly half a century, a frank and fearless exponent of the highest ideals and principles in American life, was Augustus D. Juilliard."

— NEW YORK HERALD, 1919

ABOUT

- Born April 19, 1836, at sea.
- Died April 25, 1919, New York City.
- Banker, industrialist who moved to New York in his 30s.
- Started his own textile business.
- Bequeathed fortune to musical education and opera production.
- Juilliard School of Music opened in 1924.

STARK CONNECTION

- Close friend of William McKinley.
- Grew up near Louisville.

JOHN C. DUEBER

"The Dueber-Hampden factories were at their peak of operations with 2,300 employees when John C. Dueber died in 1907. This was near-capacity for the huge buildings, which at times ran four nights a week, making a beautiful sight all lighted up."

— E.T. HEALD, AUTHOR OF "THE STARK COUNTY STORY"

ABOUT

- Born in Netphen, Germany, in 1841. His family migrated to Cincinnati.
- Started making watch cases as an apprentice.
- In 1888, Dueber bought the Hampden Watch Company in Springfield, Massachusetts, then moved it to Canton. The same year, he moved the Dueber Watch Case Company from Newport to Canton.

STARK CONNECTION

- During his company's peak, Canton was considered the watch-making capital of the world.

WILLIAM H. MARTIN

"They called me a fool — but they called Lindbergh a fool too, until he landed in Paris, and now look at what people are saying. He is the man of the hour."

— WILLIAM H. MARTIN, REFLECTING ON EARLY DEBATES ABOUT HUMAN FLIGHT.

ABOUT
- Born Jan. 21, 1855, in Canton Township.
- Died March 25, 1937, in Canton.
- Awarded patent for a single-wing airplane in 1909.
- Pulled his glider by horse, and later, by automobile.
- Wife, Almina Martin, was the first female glider pilot in the country. She also sewed cloth to the contraption's wings.
- Glider once hung in the Smithsonian next to Charles Lindbergh's "Spirit of St. Louis."

STARK CONNECTION
- Lived entire life in Canton area.
- Buried in Warstler Cemetery.
- Glider on display at MAPS Air Museum.

JOE VITALE

"You can spill a beer on me, and I'll keep playing."

ABOUT
- Born in 1949 in Canton.
- A drummer/musician, spent more than four decades recording and touring with artists such as the Eagles, Ringo Starr, John Lennon, Ted Nugent, Peter Frampton and Ronnie Wood.
- Three solo albums: 1974's "Roller Coaster Weekend," 1981's "Plantation Harbor" and 2008's "Speaking in Drums."
- Starred in the 2015 major motion picture "Ricki & The Flash" alongside Meryl Streep and Rick Springfield.

STARK CONNECTION
- A 1967 graduate of Lehman High School.

BLANCHE THEBOM

"Blanche was a huge star at one time. She was the world's leading mezzo-soprano, and she had a 22-year career at the Met, which is almost unheard of and unmatched since."

— LONGTIME FRIEND DR. ROGER GREENBERG

ABOUT
- Born Sept. 19, 1915, in Pennsylvania.
- Died at age 94 in San Francisco on March 23, 2010.
- Was a Metropolitan Opera star from 1944 to 1967.
- Gave 356 performances at the Met, playing 28 roles in 27 works.
- Appeared in films including "The Great Caruso" and "Irish Eyes are Smiling."
- Named a judge for the Miss America pageant in 1961.

STARK CONNECTION
- Grew up in Canton, where she sang in a church choir.
- Returned in 1959 to give a performance at Timken High School and earned three encores.

CHARLES R. MACAULEY

"If you look at the cartoons, the same things are happening today. It's the same tragic stuff. The same problems keep surfacing."

— JOHN SWARTZ OF PERRY TWP. ON MACAULEY

ABOUT
- Born in March 1871, in Canton.
- Died Nov. 20, 1934, in New York City.
- Pulitzer Prize-winning political cartoonist who got his start at The Repository.
- Took jobs with the Cleveland World newspaper in 1893, and the Philadelphia Inquirer in 1899. His work appeared in The Repository and publications across the country.
- Winner of 1930 Pulitzer Prize for the Brooklyn Daily Eagle.

STARK CONNECTION
- Graduate of the former Central High School.
- Worked as a sketch artist for The Repository in 1893, and at the Dueber-Hampden Watch Co.

FRANK S. LAHM

"He was a pioneer balloonist. He was an early enthusiast for development of heavier-than-aircraft. He was a connoisseur of painting. He was a successful business man. He was a distinguished social figure. He was the friend of great men."

— THE REPOSITORY, 1931

ABOUT
- Born April 25, 1846, in Canton.
- Died Dec. 29, 1931, in Paris, France.
- Son of Congressman Samuel Lahm; father of aviation pioneer Frank P. Lahm.
- Climbed the Matterhorn on Aug. 8, 1881.
- Became a balloon pilot in France in 1904.
- Crossed the Atlantic at least 50 times.
- Made last balloon flight in 1929.

STARK CONNECTION
- Founded the Aero Club of Ohio in Canton in 1907.

JOSHUA GIBBS

"Gibbs came to Ohio specifically to begin an agriculture business. He settled in Cleveland first, but decided to move to Canton in 1824. At the time, Canton and Cleveland were roughly equal in population."

— KIMBERLY KENNEY, CURATOR AT THE WM. McKINLEY PRESIDENTIAL LIBRARY & MUSEUM

ABOUT
- Born Feb. 5, 1803.
- Died Dec. 19, 1875.
- Founded Joshua Gibbs Plow Co. in 1836. It later became the Bucher & Gibbs Plow Co.
- Patented his bar share plow that same year. It sold throughout Ohio, Indiana, Michigan and Illinois.

STARK CONNECTION
- Joshua Gibbs' farmland became one of the first of several additions to the original city of Canton in the northeast.
- His plow company made Canton the first center of plow manufacturing west of the Alleghenies.

CHARITY ROTCH

In specifying the dream for her school, Rotch said the boys were to be trained in agriculture and the girls in housewifery, "whereby they may support themselves and become useful members of society."

— ROTCH'S WILL, ARCHIVED AT MASSILLON PUBLIC LIBRARY

ABOUT

- Born Oct. 31, 1766, in Newport, Rhode Island.
- Died Aug. 8, 1824, in Kendal, Ohio (now in Massillon)
- Founded a vocational boarding school for destitute orphans and the children of indigent parents, one of the first vocational schools in Ohio.
- She and her husband, Thomas, opened their home, Spring Hill, to fugitive slaves as part of the Underground Railroad.

STARK CONNECTION

- In 1811, came to Stark County with her husband seeking a milder climate to ease her frail health (as Quakers, they couldn't move farther south because of their opposition to slavery).

THE O'JAYS

"The O'Jays' story ... beginning in the late Fifties when founding members Eddie Levert and Walter Williams began singing gospel on a radio station in their hometown of Canton, Ohio. Joined by fellow high-schoolers William Powell, Bobby Massey and Bill Isles, they became the Triumphs, an R&B vocal group, in 1959."

— BIOGRAPHY BY ROCK AND ROLL HALL OF FAME AND MUSEUM

ABOUT

- An R&B group formed in 1958 in Canton.
- Original members include Eddie Levert, Walter Williams, William Powell, Bobby Massey and Bill Isles.
- Named themselves "The O'Jays" in 1963 after a Cleveland disc jockey.
- Eddie Levert and Walter Williams, who first met as children, have remained the group's constant leaders.
- Produced hits such as "Backstabbers" and "Love Train."
- Inducted into the Rock & Roll Hall of Fame in 2005.

STARK CONNECTION

- Original, lead members were raised in Canton.
- The O'Jays Parkway NE is named in their honor.

EDDIE McCLINTOCK

"The sci-fi fans tend to be pretty exuberant, and I love it."

ABOUT

- Born May 27, 1967, in Canton.
- Starred as Secret Service agent Pete Latimer on the hit SyFy network series "Warehouse 13" for five seasons, from 2009-14.
- Other acting credits include recurring roles in the TV sitcoms "Stark Raving Mad" and "Crumbs," and guest spots on "Friends," "Bones" and "Felicity."

STARK CONNECTION

- Graduated in 1985 from Hoover High School, where he wrestled and played football.
- Returned to Canton in 2013 for screening of his film "A Fish Story" at the Canton Film Festival.

CHARLES E. FIRESTONE

"Charles Firestone was another in a distinguished but vanishing group of Canton stalwarts who were in the forefront of this community's civic and business life in the 1930s and 1940s."

— EDITORIAL IN REPOSITORY ON JULY 14, 1970

ABOUT

- Born on March 10, 1890 in Plain Township.
- Died at age 80 in 1970.
- Nationally known architect who graduated from Canton's Central High School in 1908.

STARK CONNECTION

- Served as Stark County engineer from 1918-25.
- His firm designed Timken High School, former Fawcett Stadium, Canton Memorial Civic Center, the former Molly Stark Hospital and St. George Syrian Orthodox.
- Designed nearly all of the Hoover Co. buildings that were erected from 1916 until 1956 in North Canton.

HARLEY "MARTY" MULL

"His real talent was caring for his kids (he coached), the way he molded them. I don't care if you were the worst swimmer or the best swimmer, you always saw him treat them the same. … He was something special."

ABOUT

- Born July 22, 1942, in Toledo.
- Died Jan. 3, 2011 in Los Angeles.
- Owned title "fastest swimmer in the world" in early '60s.
- Helped Ohio State win an NCAA championship in 1962.
- Won back-to-back individual NCAA titles in the 200 individual medley in 1962-63, setting records each time.

STARK CONNECTION

- Set national high school records at McKinley High School from 1957 to 1960 and helped Bulldogs win four straight state championships.
- Longtime swim coach at McKinley, where he taught for 33 years.

JAMES W. LATHROP

"His liberality in contributing to public improvements and benevolent institutions was exceeded by none, if it was equaled by any."

ABOUT

- Born in 1791 in Connecticut. Died Jan. 31, 1828.
- Worked as a lawyer and held various political offices, including Ohio state legislator from 1824-27.
- Known as the "Father of Public Education" in Ohio because as a state legislator he advocated for the idea of free schools.

STARK CONNECTION

- Came to Canton in 1816 when he was 25.
- Organized Canton's first library, consisting of 30 books in 1816.
- Responsible for legislation that incorporated Canton in 1822.
- Led the movement to establish the first tax-supported schoolhouse in Canton. The two-story brick Canton Academy, which was built on the plot where the downtown campus of the McKinley High School now stands.

ANDREW CORDIER

"It should be our purpose in life to see that each of us makes such a contribution as will enable us to say that we, individually and collectively, are part of the answer to the world problem and not part of the problem itself."

ABOUT

- Born in Canton in 1901. Died on Long Island in 1975.
- Worked at U.S. State Department 1944-46.
- Executive assistant to United Nations secretaries general Trygve Lie and Dag Hammarskjold.
- Dean of School of International Affairs and president of Columbia University.
- Awarded Columbia's Alexander Hamilton Medal, the university's highest honor.

STARK CONNECTION

- Attended high school in Hartville, where he was a quarterback and valedictorian.

BEZALEEL WELLS

"Bezaleel Wells was an outstanding representative of an American system of free individual enterprise when it was least trammeled ..."

— FROM "BEZALEEL WELLS: FOUNDER OF CANTON AND STEUBENVILLE, OHIO."

ABOUT

- Born April 4, 1768.
- Eastern Ohio landowner and surveyor, created a settlement on site of the ruins of Fort Steuben, which would become the city of Steubenville in 1797.
- Although a Federalist, Wells was selected as a delegate to the constitutional convention, then as a state senator.
- Helped found Canton in 1805.

STARK CONNECTION

- Laid out the town of Canton in 1805.
- Donated land for a school, church and cemetery in Canton — the cemetery today is McKinley Park, at 501 McKinley Ave. SW.

RICHARD PAUL FINK

"As an actor, when you put on the makeup and the costume, you get to become someone else — even if it is just in the course of 2½ hours, you get to be someone else and live in another world, another time."

ABOUT

- Baritone who performs in operas worldwide.
- Started his career performing in 12 productions with the Houston Grand Opera.
- Has sung multiple premieres at the San Francisco Opera.
- Won a Grammy for best opera recording with the cast of "Doctor Atomic."

STARK CONNECTION

- Massillon native and 1973 graduate of Washington High School.
- Spent 2½ years as Obie, the school's mascot.
- Was named a Washington High School Distinguished Citizen in 2008.

JAMES B. ALLARDICE

"Not only did Allardice write the lead-ins for all 359 episodes of ("Alfred Hitchcock Presents"), he wrote many of Hitchcock's speeches during the 10 years of their collaboration."

— BIOGRAPHY ON IMDB.COM

ABOUT

- TV writer, Broadway playwright, screenwriter.
- Won the first Emmy Award for television writing.
- Head writer, "Alfred Hitchcock Presents;" other TV credits include "The Munsters,""My Three Sons," and "Gomer Pyle, USMC." Feature films: "Francis Joins the WACS," "Jumping Jacks," "At Sea With the Navy."
- His Broadway play, "At War With the Army," became a feature film starring Jerry Lewis and Dean Martin.
- Died on Feb. 15, 1966.

STARK CONNECTION

- Born in Canton, March 20, 1918.
- Repository reporter, 1941-42.

RELIENT K

"Canton will always be home. It helped shape who we are and how we sound."

— MATT THEISSEN

ABOUT

- Alternative rock band formed in 1998 in Canton by Matt Theissen, Matt Hoopes, Brian Pittman and Stephen Cushman.
- Named after Hoopes' Plymouth Reliant K car with the spelling intentionally altered to avoid trademark infringement.
- The 2004 release of album "MmHmm" catapulted the band to mainstream success.
- Grammy nominee in 2004 for Best Rock Gospel Album.
- Three certified gold albums (500,000 copies sold).

STARK CONNECTION

- Founding members attended Malone University.
- Hoopes attended McKinley, Pittman attended Perry, Theissen attended GlenOak, Cushman was home-schooled.

NICK WEATHERSPOON

"He was a good man. That's what made him so easy to talk with, to approach him. He was very humble and very approachable, and not just by me, but by anyone."

— PHIL HUBBARD, FORMER MCKINLEY AND NBA PLAYER

ABOUT

- Born July 20, 1950, in Mississippi. Died Oct. 17, 2008, in Canton.
- Played in the NBA from 1973-80 with the Washington Bullets, Seattle SuperSonics, Chicago Bulls and San Diego Clippers.
- Made NBA All-Rookie first team in 1974.
- Earned All-American honors at the University of Illinois and still holds school records for career scoring average (20.9) and rebound average (11.4).

STARK CONNECTION

- Set McKinley High School's career scoring record with 1,431 points, a mark that lasted 37 years.
- Helped the Bulldogs reach the 1969 state finals, earning first-team All-Ohio honors.

DR. MARK G. HERBST

"They filled the cars with as many people as they could jam in with no air, except for a 2-inch slit in the door. Men fought for air. This is where the veneer came off the officer and gentleman."

— HERBST ON BEING A PRISONER OF WAR DURING WORLD WAR II.

ABOUT
- Born Aug. 17, 1910, in Akron. Died May 2, 2000.
- Canton physician and war hero.
- Silver Star recipient and survivor of the 65-mile Bataan Death March during World War II.
- Major, Army Medical Corps; battalion surgeon, 3rd Battalion, 57th Infantry of the Philippine Scouts.
- Captured by the Japanese, April 13, 1942; served as prisoners' doctor, in charge of prison-camp hospital in Manchuria; liberated Aug. 17, 1945.

STARK CONNECTION
- Graduate of McKinley High School.
- President, Canton Academy of Medicine and Canton YMCA.

JOHN A. SCALI

"At times like that, a reporter has no choice. Because whatever he can do to save humanity from destruction, even just an ounce worth, he must do — and that's not just patriotic flag waving."

— ABOUT HIS INVOLVEMENT IN CUBAN MISSILE CRISIS

ABOUT
- Reporter for Boston Herald and United Press before 17 years with Associated Press. Joined ABC News in 1961.
- Played a role in diffusing the Cuban Missile Crisis in October 1962, carrying a vital message from a KGB official to U.S. officials.
- In 1971, was appointed by President Richard Nixon as a special consultant for foreign affairs and communications.
- In 1973, was named United States Representative to the United Nations.
- Died Oct. 9, 1995 at age 77.

STARK CONNECTION
- Born April 27, 1918, in Canton. McKinley High graduate.

JEAN PETERS

"The story goes that studio boss Darryl F. Zanuck took one look at the buxom green-eyed brunet and said, 'Sign her!'"

— LOS ANGELES TIMES, 2000

ABOUT

- Born Oct. 15, 1926. Died Oct. 13, 2000.
- 20th Century Fox studio actress who was a movie industry favorite in the 1950s.
- Married eccentric billionaire Howard Hughes in 1957. They divorced in 1970.
- Co-starred in films with Tyrone Power, Marilyn Monroe, Burt Lancaster, Spencer Tracy, Marlon Brando and Richard Widmark.
- Graduate of The Ohio State University.

STARK CONNECTION

- Born in Canton, raised in East Canton.

NORMA SNIPES MARCERE

"Norma Marcere, pioneer feminist and educator, is unquestionably recognized as one of the leaders of the African American Community of Stark County."

— OHIO WOMEN'S HALL OF FAME

ABOUT

- Born Oct. 21, 1908. Died Aug. 20, 2004.
- Canton's first black psychologist.
- Graduate, Kent State University; honorary doctorate, Walsh University, 1980.
- Teacher, Massillon City Schools; counselor, Akron City Schools; psychologist, Kent City Schools.
- Founder of PAX, the St. Mary's Project for Academic Excellence Saturday School, and the STRIVE study program.
- Inductee, Ohio Women's Hall of Fame, Canton YWCA Stark County Women's Hall of Fame, Stark County Wall of Fame; 1973 Junior League Woman of the Year.

STARK CONNECTION

- Born in Canton. McKinley High School graduate.

HENRY MITCHELL

"Henry Mitchell was a most unusual sculptor, and his success as a creator of public animal monuments is due in no small measure to the tastes and traditions of the most unusual city of Philadelphia."

— EDWARD F. FRY

ABOUT

- Studied economics at Princeton.
- Had a corporate career before leaving his hometown of Canton to pursue art.
- Attended Temple University's Tyler School of Art.
- Studied with Marino Marini in Milan, where he kept a studio and used foundries for many of his sculptures.
- Was well-known in the Philadelphia art scene, particularly for abstract and animal sculptures, from the 1950s until his death in 1980.

STARK CONNECTION

- Born in Canton in 1915.
- Crafted the bronze Pegasus at Canton Cultural Center.

DALE RAYMOND WRIGHT

"As a pioneering African-American journalist, Mr. Wright integrated the newsroom of the now-defunct New York World Telegram and Sun, where he wrote articles that made him a finalist for the Pulitzer Prize, American journalism's highest honor. He was also one of the first African-Americans to graduate from Ohio State University's journalism school."

— THE RIVERDALE PRESS, 2009

ABOUT

- Born in Monongahela, Pennsylvania, he was an award-winning journalist, author and businessman who also was a World War II Marine veteran.
- Graduate of The Ohio State University; associate editor, Jet and Ebony; reporter, New York World Telegram and Sun.
- 1962 Pulitzer Prize finalist for an under-cover series on migrant workers.
- Director of public relations for New York City Mayor Ed Koch, Sen. Jacob Javits and Gov. Nelson Rockefeller.
- Died in New York City, 2009.

STARK CONNECTION

- 1941 McKinley High School alumnus.

FRANK P. LAHM

"Lt. Lahm is a prince among gentleman and a gentleman among aeronauts."

— ALAN R. HOWLEY, WINNER OF THE 1910 GORDON BENNETT CUP, IN JULY 1911.

ABOUT

- Born Nov. 17, 1877, in Mansfield. Died July 7, 1963, in Sandusky.
- 1901 graduate of West Point Academy.
- Served in the military from 1901-41, rising through the ranks in the U.S. Army, U.S. Signal Corps, Air Service and Army Air Corps.
- On Oct. 26, 1909, became the world's first military aviator — the first pilot certified by the U.S. Army. In 1919, piloted the first U.S. Army airship, becoming the only military officer licensed to fly a balloon, dirigible and airplane.
- Known as "the father of Air Force flight training."
- Retired as brigadier general in the Army Air Corps on Nov. 20, 1914, just weeks before the U.S. involvement in World War I. He offered to return to service, but his request was denied.

STARK CONNECTION

- The son of Frank S. Lahm, balloonist and founder of the Canton-based Aero Club of Ohio.

LOUIS SCHAEFER

"Schaefer tended to like people in the entertainment business and they liked him. Many well-known actors of the period brought their plays to Canton, though they often overlooked other towns of similar size. As a result, Cantonians were able to see first-rate theatrical productions."

— KIMBERLY KENNEY, CURATOR WM. MCKINLEY PRESIDENTIAL LIBRARY & MUSEUM

ABOUT

- Born Dec. 25, 1815, in France. Died 1889.
- Opened Schaefer's Opera House in 1868 in Canton.
- Studied law at Griswold and Grant in Canton.
- Lobbied for more brick-paved streets and a new county courthouse. He also brought the first steam engine to Canton (nicknamed Schaefer) and helped create a city water system.
- Atheist who antagonized the community's religious by scheduling popular performances at the opera house during church services.

STARK CONNECTION

- Came to Stark County in 1830 when his parents moved to America.

JOHN SHORB

"The remnants of the oak tree, the site of the early Catholic Masses on Shorb's farm, were made into a chair, now on display at Basilica of St. John the Baptist."

— HISTORY OF BASILICA OF ST. JOHN THE BAPTIST

ABOUT

- Born about 1758 in Zweibrücken, Rheinpfalz, Germany. Died July 24, 1824, in Canton.
- He and his family credited with bringing Catholicism to Canton, hosted city's first Mass in 1817. Masses often celebrated beneath oak tree on family farm (now Fifth Street and High Avenue NW).
- Donated 5 acres of land for Catholic church, which today is Basilica of St. John the Baptist at 627 McKinley Ave. NW.
- Moved to Canton in 1807, friends with city founder Bezaleel Wells. Shorb and Wells loved trees, which is why downtown streets often were named after a tree.

STARK CONNECTION

- Opened city's first grocery store and became president of first bank, Farmer's Bank.
- Died tragically when struck by a falling timber during construction of the original St. John Catholic Church.

LEN DAWSON

"If Leonard doesn't come to Dallas, we don't win the (AFL) Championship. If we don't move to Kansas City, maybe we don't have a merger (between the AFL-NFL)."

— HANK STRAM, ON LEN DAWSON'S IMPACT ON PRO FOOTBALL

ABOUT

- Born June 20, 1935, in Alliance.
- Enshrined in the Pro Football Hall of Fame, Class of 1987, after a 19-year career in the AFL and NFL, including 14 years with the Dallas Texans/Kansas City Chiefs.
- Started at quarterback for the Chiefs in the first Super Bowl, a 35-10 loss to the Packers.
- Led the Chiefs to a 23-7 win in Super Bowl IV, earning MVP.
- Hosted HBO's "Inside the NFL" for 23 seasons.
- Led Big Ten in passing for three seasons at Purdue.

STARK CONNECTION

- Earned All-Ohio honors at Alliance High School in football and basketball
- Inducted into the Stark County High School Football Hall of Fame as part of the inaugural class in 2002.

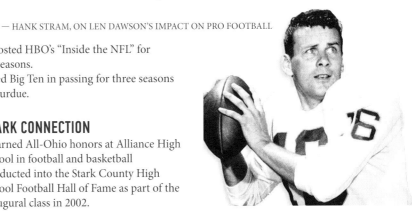

ELIZABETH AULTMAN HARTER

"If (Cornelius Aultman's widow and his daughter) had not established Canton's first hospital in his honor in 1892 — The Aultman Memorial Hospital — the great name of Aultman would no longer be very visible."

— RICHARD HALDI, AUTHOR OF "CORNELIUS AULTMAN: OHIO'S GREAT CIVIL-WAR-ERA INDUSTRIALIST"

ABOUT

- Born May 14, 1847, in Lake Township. Died Oct. 25, 1932, in Canton.
- Daughter of industrialist Cornelius Aultman, who became one of the richest men of his time.
- Wife of George D. Harter, one of Canton's leading bankers. At least five presidents were overnight guests at their home.

STARK CONNECTION

- In 1891, she and her stepmother donated 4.5 acres of land to build the city's first hospital as a lasting memorial to her father. Aultman Hospital opened Jan. 17, 1892. The Aultman School of Nursing opened that same year.

JOHN CHAPMAN

"Johnny Appleseed's name will never be forgotten. ... We will keep his memory green, and future generations of boys and girls will love him as we, who knew him, have learned to love him."

— GEN. TECUMSAH SHERMAN IN HIS EULOGY OF CHAPMAN

ABOUT

- Better known as Johnny Appleseed, the legendary nomadic pioneer who brought apple trees to Ohio, Pennsylvania, Indiana, Illinois, West Virginia and Ontario, Canada.
- Born in Leominster, Mass., on Sept. 26, 1774; died March 18, 1845, in Fort Wayne, Ind.
- Contrary to the myth, he actually bought land to plant nurseries and left them in the care of a neighbor, returning every few years to tend to the trees.

STARK CONNECTION

- Planted the first orchard in Perry Township on the Daum Estate.
- Frequent visitor in the Stark County area; bought land for a nursery in 1809 on the corner of Cleveland Avenue and 5th Street in Canton.

IORWITH W. ABEL

"One of the greatest there ever was. He was very effective. A lot of changes came under his administration. He was sort of a world leader."

— DANIEL SCIURY, PRESIDENT OF HALL OF FAME CENTRAL LABOR COUNCIL AFL-CIO

ABOUT

- Born Aug. 11, 1908. Died Aug. 10, 1987.
- Helped found the United Steelworkers of America, and served as president from 1965 to 1977.
- Served on the Kerner Commission, which compiled a federal study of urban riots during the late 1960s.
- Signed the Experimental Negotiating Agreement with the major steel corporations in 1973. With this agreement, most local union presidents agreed not to strike during the 1974 contract negotiations.

STARK CONNECTION

- Graduate of Magnolia High School, attended Canton Actual Business College
- Worked at Timken Co. and Canton Malleable Iron Co.

BOZ SCAGGS

"I'm still trying to re-create a Ray Charles concert that I heard when I was 15 years old, and all my nerve endings were fried and transformed, and electricity shot through me."

ABOUT

- Gained fame in '60s as guitarist and one-time lead singer with Steve Miller Band.
- Scored several solo top 20 singles in U.S., including "Lowdown" and "Lido Shuffle."
- Album "Silk Degrees" reached No. 2 on U.S. Billboard 200 and No. 1 in numerous other countries, selling more than 5 million copies.
- In 2015, released "A Fool to Care," a compilation of mainly cover songs, including pieces with Lucinda Williams and Bonnie Raitt.

STARK CONNECTION

- Born June 8, 1944, in Canton.

PEGGY ANN GARNER

"By the time she reached 20, she had moved from Hollywood to New York to try her talents on Broadway. She spent much of the 1950s living and working in New York, studying with The Actors Studio. She appeared on stage with Dorothy Gish in 'The Man' in 1950. She received Harvard University's Hasty Pudding Award for 'Woman of the Year' in 1956."

— BIOGRAPHY ON IMDB.COM

ABOUT

- Academy Award winner (juvenile) for her 1945 starring role in "A Tree Grows in Brooklyn."
- Other films include "Jane Eyre," "Keys of the Kingdom," and "Junior Miss."
- Became a game-show panelist and stage and episodic TV actress as an adult. Also went into the real-estate business.
- The whereabouts of her Oscar unknown.
- Died Oct. 16, 1984.

STARK CONNECTION

- Born in Canton on Feb. 3, 1932.

JEFF TIMMONS

"I think our mentality was we just want to keep getting songs on the radio. We don't have time to say, 'Well, we're cooler, we're hotter, we're better looking than Backstreet Boys and NSync.' We just want what they've got. Song after song after song. Hit after hit after hit."

ABOUT

- Born April 23, 1973, in Canton.
- Founding member of pop group 98 Degrees.
- Band's album "98 Degrees and Rising" went four times platinum in 1998, and the band has sold more than 10 million records overall.
- Scored a No. 1 hit single and Grammy nomination for "Thank God I Found You," a collaboration with Mariah Carey and Joseph "Joe" Thomas.

STARK CONNECTION

- 1991 graduate of Massillon Washington High School.
- Attended Malone University.

33

JACK PAAR

"I kid you not."

— THE PHRASE JACK PAAR UTTERED ON "THE TONIGHT SHOW," PRIOR
TO LAUNCHING INTO A COMICAL ANECDOTE ABOUT HIS LIFE OR FAMILY.

ABOUT

- Born May 1, 1918, in Canton. Died Jan. 27, 2004
- Took over for Steve Allen in 1957 as the second host of "The Tonight Show," on NBC.
- Famously walked off the set in 1960 after network censor edited one of his jokes. He left the show for good in 1962 and was replaced by Johnny Carson.
- Credited with revolutionizing late-night TV, creating the talk show format and opening monologue.

STARK CONNECTION

- Although he was born in Canton, he largely grew up in Michigan. His father, Howard, worked for the New York Central Railroad, so the Paar family often moved.

CHARLES CLEWELL

"It's a real thrill to make a delicate precision part and find that it meets perfectly with specifications measured in millionths of an inch."

— CHARLES WALTER CLEWELL ON BEING A TOOLMAKER FOR THE TIMKEN ROLLER BEARING CO.

ABOUT

- Born 1876. Died 1965.
- Spent 50 years studying, experimenting and perfecting the process of producing exotic creations in bronze.
- Retired toolmaker for The Timken Roller Bearing Co.
- Veteran of the Spanish-American War.
- Awarded the Diploma de Medaille d'Argent from the French government as a tribute to an exhibit of his work at the 1937 Paris International Exposition.

STARK CONNECTION

- Lived with daughter at 152 18th St. NW
- Was an honorary member of the Canton Art Institute (Canton Museum of Art).

SAMUEL BEATTY

"With pride I mention the name of Brig. Gen. Samuel Beatty for his conduct on this occasion."

— COMMANDER THOMAS L. CRITTENDEN WHEN RECOUNTING BEATTY'S PERSONAL BRAVERY AT THE BATTLE OF CHICKAMAUGA IN SEPTEMBER 1863.

ABOUT

- Born Dec. 16, 1820, in Pennsylvania. Died May 25, 1885, in Jackson Township.
- Formed a volunteer Civil War unit — Co. A of the 19th Ohio Infantry, called the "Canton Light Guards" — and became the regiment's first colonel.
- In 1865, promotion to brevet grade of major general of the volunteers made him the highest-ranking Union Army officer from Stark County.

STARK CONNECTION

- Elected Stark County sheriff in 1857, serving two two-year terms.
- Buried in Massillon City Cemetery.

FRANK T. BOW

"In over 20 years of outstanding service in Congress, Frank Bow earned respect as a man of energy, principle and dedication."

— PRESIDENT RICHARD NIXON ON THE DEATH OF FRANK T. BOW ON NOV. 13, 1972

ABOUT

- Born Feb. 20, 1901. Died on Nov. 13, 1972.
- In 1929, appointed assistant attorney general of Ohio.
- Served as an overseas radio correspondent for WHBC during World War II, covering combat in the Philippines.
- In 1950, elected to the U.S. House of Representatives and was considered an ardent supporter of tax reform.
- Retired from Congress in 1972 and was set to become the U.S. ambassador to Panama prior to his death.
- The Frank T. Bow Federal Building is named in his honor in downtown Canton.

STARK CONNECTION

- Born in Canton and returned to the city to practice law.

REUBEN KLAMER

"When I was a kid, I loved the Game of Life. It was my favorite game. It is exciting its inventor is from Canton. He donated the 25th edition (in a silver box on exhibit in the Children's Corner) to the museum."

— KIMBERLY KENNEY, CURATOR, WM. MCKINLEY PRESIDENTIAL LIBRARY & MUSEUM

ABOUT

- Born June 18, 1922
- Game designer and toy game inventor famous for creating the Game of Life.
- Invented 200 other toys, including the Spin-A-Hoop to compete with Wham-O's Hula Hoop, Gaylord the Walking Dog and Busy Blocks.
- Inducted into the Toy Industry Hall of Fame in 2005.
- Produced gadgets for such shows as "The Man From U.N.C.L.E." and "Star Trek." His phaser rifle was used in the "Where No Man Has Gone Before" episode of "Star Trek."

STARK CONNECTION

- Canton native.
- 1940 McKinley High School graduate.

JANET WEIR CREIGHTON

"When the sales tax rolls around again, we've got a lot of 'splaining to do, as Lucy used to say."

— STARK COUNTY COMMISSIONER JANET WEIR CREIGHTON IN 2014 COMMENTING ON RAISES FOR COUNTY EMPLOYEES THAT WERE DOUBLE WHAT THE COMMISSIONERS RECOMMENDED.

ABOUT

- Born Aug. 22, 1950, at Aultman Hospital in Canton.
- White House deputy assistant to President George W. Bush and director of intergovernmental affairs from 2008 to 2009.
- Republican National Convention delegate or alternate 1996, 2000, 2004 and 2012. Convention whip in 1996 and 2000. National GOP Platform Committee co-chair in 2004.

STARK CONNECTION

- Graduated from Canton Lincoln High School in 1968.
- Stark County recorder from 1985 to 1991.
- Stark County Auditor from 1991 to 2003.
- Canton mayor from 2004 to 2007.
- Stark County commissioner from 2011 to present.

GUY TILDEN

"He was a skillful, versatile and prolific architect whose designs incorporated an acute attention to ornamental detail and an ability to blend the romantic touches of older eras with modern construction technology in a full range of building types."

— CANTON PRESERVATION SOCIETY IN AN APPLICATION TO THE NATIONAL REGISTER OF HISTORIC PLACES.

ABOUT

- Born May 11, 1858, in Youngstown. Died Aug. 6, 1929, in Canton.
- Canton's premier architect from the mid-1880s until his retirement in 1924.
- Named a fellow of the American Institute of Architects in 1889.
- Designed at least 50 buildings in Canton, from factories and offices to schools and private homes.
- Many of his buildings have been placed on the National Register of Historic Places, including Trinity Lutheran Church in Canton; Benders Tavern in Canton; and the former Canton Public Library.

STARK CONNECTION

- Moved to Alliance in 1880, then to Canton in 1883.
- Buried in West Lawn Cemetery.

BENJAMIN F. FAIRLESS

"Clearly, this was an important figure in American industry in the middle of the 20th century and later on in the century."

— BRADY SMITH OF THE HEINZ HISTORY CENTER IN PITTSBURGH

ABOUT

- Born May 3, 1890, in Pigeon Run area of southwestern Stark County. Died Jan. 1, 1962.
- President of U.S. Steel Corp. from 1938 to 1952; chairman and chief executive officer from 1952 to 1955; and oversaw U.S. Steel's modernization and expansion.
- Received Medal for Merit civilian award in 1946 for helping break the steel production bottleneck during World War II.

STARK CONNECTION

- Class valedictorian at Justus High in Stark County in 1905.
- Fairless Local School District in southwestern Stark County was named in his honor when the school system was created in 1956.

ERIC SNOW

"I just felt like it was a privilege to do it and to be a part of a tradition and history (at McKinley). When I had an opportunity to do it, it felt great. It felt like it was something you want to be a part of. It's long gone, but I still take pride in being a McKinley Bulldog and a Canton Ohioan forever."

— SNOW ON PLAYING FOR MCKINLEY

ABOUT
- Born April 24, 1973, in Canton.
- Played in the NBA for 13 seasons. Played in the NBA Finals with the Sonics, Sixers and Cavs.
- Received NBA's J. Walter Kennedy Citizenship Award in 2005 and the NBA Sportsmanship Award in 2000.
- After retirement, went into broadcasting, then coaching, and now is an assistant coach at Florida Atlantic.

STARK CONNECTION
- Starred at McKinley High School, earning first team All-Ohio honors as a junior and senior.
- Donated $1 million in 2012 to help with the construction of new Canton YMCA, which now bears his name.

CHARLES L. BABCOCK

"(He) was fond of (President Kennedy). Everywhere he went in Ohio, my dad went."

— JAMES BABCOCK, SON OF CHARLES BABCOCK

ABOUT
- Served as Canton's mayor from 1958-61
- Instrumental in updating city's water system with construction of Sugar Creek facility in Tuscarawas County.
- Among three city water plants, Sugar Creek opened in 1962, with the capacity to provide millions of gallons per day from an underground water source.
- A new City Hall building was constructed during his time as mayor and stands today.
- Attended inaugural ball of President John F. Kennedy.
- Died in 1972.

STARK CONNECTION
- Canton native.

JOHN McTAMMANY

"This was a man who had been involved in the player industry for nearly all his working life, and who felt so strongly that he had been wronged, that he wrote two lengthy books in order to explain his priority over other inventors."

— THE PIANOLA INSTITUTE

ABOUT

- Born June 26, 1845, in Glasgow, Scotland.
- Claimed to be the original inventor of the mechanical player piano.
- Battled others who also had patents to manufacture the invention.
- Wrote two books, "History of the Player" and "The Technical History of the Player."
- Invented a voting machine based on perforated paper.

- Died March 26, 1915, in Stamford, Connecticut.

STARK CONNECTION

- Moved to United States in 1862 and settled in the Uniontown area of Lake Township.

IRVING BARNES

"The youth is an actor of rare gifts for comedy and his versatility in reading all the parts from the gently austere role of 'De Lawd' to that of the rebellious, jazz singing young Seba."

— 1941 REPOSITORY STORY ABOUT BARNES IN "THE GREEN PASTURES"

GERSHWIN
PORGY AND BESS
(extraits célèbres)
IRVING BARNES - LEESA FORSTER
CŒURS ET ORCHESTRE DU CONCERTHALL, HAAR
LORENZO FULLER

ABOUT

- Born in 1923.
- Became a popular baritone on radio and television.
- Performed in numerous Broadway musicals, including "Porgy and Bess," between 1947 and 1985.
- Sang with the New York Philharmonic Symphony and the Pittsburgh Opera.

STARK CONNECTION

- Attended South Market School in Canton, graduated from McKinley High School in 1941.
- Won a national title in humorous declamation in 1941.
- Started a weekly series of song programs that aired on WHBC in 1941.

HARRY H. INK

"The only orchard that I know where every tiny detail has been looked after regardless of expense is the one at Canton, O., belonging to H.H. Ink. Mr. Ink started a good many years ago dreaming about an orchard. His financial success in other lines has enabled him to make his dream come true."

— BENJAMIN WALLACE DOUGLASS, ONE OF THE HIGHEST PAID HORTICULTURAL WRITERS IN THE WORLD, IN 1923

ABOUT

- Born Aug. 29, 1864 in Clarksville, Pa. Died in 1926.
- Left home at age 17 to go to Leetonia, Ohio, to work in a drug store owned by his father. Became a registered pharmacist who invented Tonsiline, a throat gargle.

STARK CONNECTION

- Came to Canton in 1891 and bought a drug store on Tuscarawas Street. Sold the store to two clerks, and it became the first Roth & Hug store.
- Financed construction of Canton Palace Theatre.
- Planted 12,500 trees in 1914 along Fulton Road, creating Aplink Orchards.
- Namesake of Ink Park on Park Drive NW in Canton.

ORVILLE N. HARTSHORN

"(He) understood the important role education could play in the development of our country and its people. And he wanted to extend educational opportunity to those most in need of it. Founding Mount Union in 1846, he proclaimed his commitment to educate students. He also endorsed co-education. We try, each day, to uphold and advance his bold vision."

— RICHARD MERRIMAN JR., PRESIDENT OF UNIVERSITY OF MOUNT UNION

ABOUT

- Born Aug. 20, 1823, in Portage County. Died Sept. 17, 1901.
- In 1846, opened what became Mount Union College with six students.
- Had the goal of launching a college where higher education would be offered to all people regardless of race.
- Was a Methodist minister and established the practice of Bible readings and chapel exercises at Mount Union.

STARK CONNECTION

- Arrived from Meadville, Pennsylvania, to what was known as the Village of Mount Union in 1846 to visit a gravely ill sister. Mount Union residents requested Hartshorn start a school there. He had been an educator.

CURVIS F. RHYNE

"From a local standpoint, he was the ultimate politician. The goal of a politician is to get elected. He took care of his constituents. Alliance lost a great politician and the black community lost a great friend in Curvis."

— FORMER ALLIANCE MUNI. COURT JUDGE MICHAEL TANGI

ABOUT

- Born Aug. 25, 1922, in Georgia. Died Aug. 24, 2007.
- Served 48 consecutive years as a member of Alliance City Council.
- Longtime member of the Stark County Community Action Agency board of directors.
- One of the founders of Alliance Negro History Club.

STARK CONNECTION

- One of the longest tenures as a municipal councilman on Alliance City Council. At the time of departure from Alliance City Council at the end of 1999, he represented the city's 1st Ward.

RICHARD "DICK" McFARLAND

"One of the finest netters ever produced in this area, McFarland had no superior during his tenure as champion. Possessed of a full bag of shots, Dick plays a cool and collected game, mixing a powerful forehand drive with a superb backhand and uncanny placement shots."

— THE REPOSITORY, 1946

ABOUT

- Born Feb. 29, 1916, in Byesville, moved to Canton at age 9.
- Family name was McFarlane but attending physician wrote a "d" instead of an "e" at the end, and it stuck.
- Starred in tennis at McKinley High School in the mid-1930s, and was a top player at Ohio State University.
- Was a nationally ranked tennis player.

STARK CONNECTION

- Developed the city recreation department tennis competitions and revived the Canton City School District tennis program. A physical education teacher in the district's elementary schools, McFarland simultaneously coached tennis at all four city high schools and ran the city's annual tennis tournament.

DAVID CANARY

"There's a great deal of child in me and acting is fun. It's a make-believe thing."

ABOUT
- Born Aug. 25, 1938. Died Nov. 16, 2015.
- Rose to prominence playing Candy in the Western TV series "Bonanza," 1967-73.
- Starred on "All My Children" from 1983-2010.
- Won five Daytime Emmy Awards and 11 additional nominations for "All My Children."
- A baritone vocalist, Canary starred in such stage musicals as "Man of La Mancha," "Sweeney Todd" and "Carousel."

STARK CONNECTION
- Grew up in Massillon.
- Has a street named after him, David Canary Drive SW.

TODD BLACKLEDGE

"The Six W's: Work will win when wishing won't."

ABOUT
- Born Feb. 25, 1961, in Canton.
- Starting quarterback for three years at Penn State, helping the Nittany Lions win a national title in the 1982 season when he won the Davey O'Brien Award as the nation's top QB.
- Played in the National Football League for seven seasons between 1983-89 for the Kansas City Chiefs and Pittsburgh Steelers.
- Started his broadcasting career in sports talk radio before working as a football analyst for Big East, ESPN, ABC and CBS sports networks.

STARK CONNECTION
- Son of Stark County native and former NFL assistant coach Ron Blackledge. Played sports and graduated from Hoover High School.
- Lives in North Canton, coaches Hoover High School basketball.

PAUL ALLMAN SIPLE

"He went south with us as a Boy Scout, but he took his place as a man."

— ADMIRAL RICHARD BYRD ABOUT SIPLE'S FIRST TRIP TO ANTARCTICA

ABOUT

- Born Dec. 18, 1908, in Montpelier, Ohio. Died Nov. 25, 1968.
- American explorer and geographer who took several Antarctic expeditions, including two (one as an Eagle Scout) with Richard Byrd.
- Devised the Wind Chill Index, which measures how wind speed affects the rate of heat loss, as a result of a trip to the South Pole.
- Memorialized with geographical features bearing his name, including Siple Island, Mount Siple and the Siple Coast in Antarctica.

STARK CONNECTION

- Canton was an adopted home, and, between exploration trips to the South Pole, he made frequent extended trips to the city to visit his sister, Carol Siple Kettering, and her husband, Lester.
- Siple's mother lived in Canton for 20 years.

JOSEPH MEDILL

"What's the news?"

— MEDILL'S LAST WORDS, AS LEGEND HAS IT

ABOUT

- Born April 6, 1823, in Canada. Died March 16, 1899.
- Published newspapers in Coshocton and Cleveland before owning and editing the Chicago Tribune.
- Served two years as mayor of Chicago and was key in the founding of the Chicago Public Library.
- Family endowed Medill School of Journalism at Northwestern University.

STARK CONNECTION

- Medill's family moved to a farm in Pike Township in 1837, and Medill came to Canton in 1844 to study law.
- Worked for Repository founder John Saxton "writing the mail," or rewriting incoming newspaper exchanges and the news of interest in Canton. Also learned from Saxton how to set type.

WILLIAM J. POWELL

"The only color that matters is the color of the greens."

ABOUT

- Born Nov. 22, 1916. Died Dec. 31, 2009, in Canton.
- Banned from all-white public courses, he was rejected for a loan to build his own. Then bought 78-acre dairy farm in East Canton, which he opened in 1948 as the integrated Clearview Golf Club.
- Was the first African American to design, construct and own a professional golf course in the United States.
- Inducted into the National Black Golf Hall of Fame.

STARK CONNECTION

- In his youth, lived in Minerva and later Canton.
- His daughter, Renee Powell, is a veteran golf pro who serves as Clearview Golf Club's head professional.

NELL DORR

"The best part of the day was in the evening after supper when Papa and I would go into the darkroom. We would close the door and enter a magical world."

ABOUT

- Born Aug. 27, 1893, Cleveland.
- In 1931, she set up a studio in New York City, where her Massillon childhood friend, actress Lillian Gish, introduced her to the subjects for her Portraits of Famous Men exhibition.
- She is best remembered for her photography books, most notably "Mother and Child," 1954.
- In 1983, the Corcoran Gallery of Art in Washington, D.C., included her work in an exhibition of 10 great women in photography.
- Died Nov. 15, 1988, in Washington, Connecticut.

STARK CONNECTION

- Nell learned "the magic of the darkroom" at her father's side in the Jacob Becker Photography Studio near the current site of the Massillon Museum.
- In 1938, Dorr donated 18 of her fine art prints to the Massillon Museum, which has several times exhibited her work, most recently in the 2010 exhibition, "Between Two Worlds."

BRANNON BRAGA

"I complain bitterly on a daily basis that I'm too busy, but I don't know what I would do otherwise. Filmmaking, I'm so lucky to be doing it. It's my passion. On the other hand, if my showbiz career went away tomorrow, I don't have any other skills at all."

ABOUT

- Born Aug. 14, 1965, in Bozeman, Montana.
- A television producer, director and screenwriter who most recently served as an executive producer on the Fox primetime series "Cosmos: A Spacetime Odyssey."
- Served as executive producer and writer on Fox shows "24" and "Terra Nova."
- Served as executive producer for the series

"Star Trek: The Next Generation," "Star Trek: Voyager" and "Star Trek: Enterprise," and he also co-wrote the feature films "Star Trek: Generations" and "Star Trek: First Contact."

STARK CONNECTION

- 1983 McKinley High School graduate.

HENRY S. FINKENBINER

He won the Medal of Honor "for a heroic charge in the Civil War."

— STARS AND STRIPES, SEPT. 7, 2011

ABOUT

- Congressional Medal of Honor recipient during the Civil War.
- Crossed the millrace on a burning bridge and determined the enemy's position while he was on the advance skirmish line and in close range of the enemy's artillery on April 9, 1865, in Dingles Mill, S.C.
- Served in the Union Army in Company D, 107th Ohio Infantry.

STARK CONNECTION

- Born July 29, 1842, in North Industry to George and Susannah Stands Finkenbiner.
- Died June 3, 1922, at age 80 in Danville, Ill.
- His father was a blacksmith by trade.
- The family lived in the village then called Sparta.

ROSE BAMPTON

"A tall classic figure with distant dreamy eyes, the white oval face of some antique statue, utter repose, soft brown hair waving across a wide brow."

— OPERA NEWS, 1942

ABOUT

- Born Nov. 28, 1907, Lakewood. Died Aug. 21, 2007.
- On her 25th birthday, she made her debut with the New York Metropolitan Opera, where she starred for 18 seasons.
- She performed for Franklin D. Roosevelt and Dwight D. Eisenhower's White House guests, sang the national anthem for the opening of the 1939 World's Fair and performed a radio duet with Humphrey Bogart.

STARK CONNECTION

- Bampton and her family lived in Massillon next to the Woodland Avenue SW home where the Gish sisters often stayed with their aunt.

RICHARD MILLER

"Art is dependent on beauty and truth, not on imitation and pretense."

ABOUT

- Born April 9, 1926. Died May 5, 2009.
- Taught voice five years at the University of Michigan and 42 years at the Oberlin Conservatory of Music.
- Wrote eight books about singing.
- Was awarded a Fulbright grant to study voice in Rome.
- Performed as leading lyric tenor at opera house in Zurich, Switzerland; also performed with San Francisco Opera.

STARK CONNECTION

- Performed often in Canton area before his voice changed at age 11.
- Graduated from Lincoln High School, where he performed in musicals.

JOSEPH G. HARNER

"For extraordinary heroism in the line of his profession during the seizure of Vera Cruz, Mexico, 21 April 1914."

— THE MEDAL OF HONOR AWARD CITATION

ABOUT

- Vera Cruz Congressional Medal of Honor recipient during the Mexican campaign in 1914.
- Boatswain's Mate, 2nd Class in the U.S. Navy serving on the U.S.S. Florida (right) on April 21, 1914, when he became a member of the landing party taking part in control of the city during the Siege of Vera Cruz, Mexico.
- An excellent marksman, he shot one of the most revered Mexican national heroes — Lt. Jose Azueta — from 300 yards in the heat of battle.
- He also served with honor in World War I and World War II.
- Died March 5, 1958. Buried in Arlington National Cemetery.

STARK CONNECTION

- Born Feb. 19, 1889, in Louisville.

USS FLORIDA (BB 30)

CAROLINE McCULLOUGH EVERHARD

"As was natural in a woman of broad mind, excellent judgment and great mental force, Mrs. Everhard occupied a number of positions of trust and confidence in the community."

— THE EVENING INDEPENDENT

ABOUT

- Born Sept. 14, 1843, Massillon. Died April 14, 1902, Massillon.
- In 1890, she was elected president of the Ohio Suffrage Association, a post she held for 10 years, working with national suffrage leaders.
- During her tenure and largely due to her leadership, Ohio women earned school suffrage, became eligible to serve on school boards, and gained the right to vote in municipal elections.

STARK CONNECTION

- Became the first female bank director in Ohio, at Massillon's Union Bank, in 1885.
- Incorporator of the McClymonds Public Library Association (now Massillon Public Library) and an active board member of Charity School of Kendal.

LOUISE TIMKEN

"There is no greater champion of worthy aviation causes than Louise Timken."

— PIMA AIR & SPACE MUSEUM, ARIZONA AVIATION HALL OF FAME

ABOUT

- Born in 1910 in Cleveland. Died Oct. 3, 1998, at home in Canton.
- Worked with sister-in-law Mary Timken to establish the Cultural Center for the Arts in Canton, a major project of The Timken Foundation.
- Began flying in 1943 and was a active member of the Civil Air Patrol during World War II.

- In 1958, became the first woman in the United States to fly and own a jet aircraft.
- The first woman to receive a type rating in a Lear jet and owned one of the first models built in 1965.

STARK CONNECTION

- Married Henry H. Timken Jr.
- Longtime member and past president of the Akron-Canton Airport board.

RAY DENCZAK

"Had I had known in World War II that there would be a misuse of the First Amendment by the newspaper (The Repository) ... I would have surrendered to the Germans by saying, 'Comrade.' "

— DENCZAK, WHO IN 2005 EXPRESSED HIS ANGER AT A REPOSITORY ILLUSTRATION THAT PLACED LIKENESSES OF CANDIDATES WHO HAD LOST THE ELECTION IN AN IMAGE OF CRUMPLED PHOTOGRAPHS TOSSED INTO A TRASH CAN.

ABOUT

- Born Jan. 4, 1925 in Canton. Died Sept. 6, 2006.
- Served in the Army Air Force in World War II.
- Worked 35 years at Ford Motor Company as a design engineer.

STARK CONNECTION

- After serving as fourth ward councilman for two years in the early 1960s, Canton Council president from 1972 to 1987 and 1990 to Sept. 9, 2006.
- Lost in his bid for mayor in 1987 after Sam Purses, the eventual mayor, defeated him in the Democratic primary.

LARRY SNYDER

"He gets more out of you than you ever dreamed you had. ... At the Olympic Games, he had me so fired up I couldn't miss."

— OLYMPIC LEGEND JESSE OWENS ON SNYDER

ABOUT
- Won the Western Conference Medal for scholarship and track achievements at The Ohio State University, from which he graduated in 1925.
- Hired as head track coach at Ohio State in 1932, coached Jesse Owens, Glenn Davis and Gene Albritto. Led 15 athletes to Olympic medals.
- Head coach of the U.S. Track and Field Team for 1960 Rome Olympics.
- Coached at Ohio State until 1965. His athletes were named All-American 52 times and set 14 world records.
- Inducted into the USA Track & Field Hall of Fame in 1978.
- Died Sept. 25, 1982.

STARK CONNECTION
- Born Aug. 9, 1896 in Canton.

JOSH McDANIELS

"He is a phenomenal coach. He is so prepared, he's so smart, he's a great leader for us as an offense, and I trust him implicitly with everything that he designs, schemes up."

— PATRIOTS STAR QUARTERBACK TOM BRADY TALKING ABOUT McDANIELS PRIOR TO SUPER BOWL XLIX

ABOUT
- Born April 21, 1976.
- Won four Super Bowl rings as an assistant with New England.
- 2016 was his eighth year as New England's offensive coordinator and his 13th season overall as a Patriots assistant, having worked there from 2001-08 and returning in 2012.
- Served as head coach of the Denver Broncos in 2009 and part of 2010.
- Helped guide 2007 Patriots to NFL records for points scored and TDs.

STARK CONNECTION
- Played quarterback and kicked for McKinley High School from 1992-94, helping the Bulldogs reach the playoffs his junior and senior years and winning a regional title in 1994.
- His father, Thom, served as McKinley's head coach from 1982-97.

49

LEWIS MILLER

"If it weren't for Miller, we'd have one less Elvis movie."

— JOANNA MILLER IN A 2015 ESSAY IN "AKRON EMPIRE" NEWSPAPER, NOTING
THAT PRESLEY APPEARED IN A FILM ABOUT A TRAVELING CHAUTAUQUA TENT SHOW.

ABOUT

- Born in Greentown on July 24, 1829. Died in 1899.
- Industrialist and philanthropist.
- Invented the Buckeye Mower and held 92 patents, mostly for farm machinery.
- Designed the "Akron Plan," a design for Sunday school classrooms.
- Co-founded what became Mount Union College.
- Was Thomas Edison's father-in-law.

STARK CONNECTION

- Was stepbrother of Cornelius Aultman and organized and built the Akron factory for Aultman Co.
- Co-founded Canton Electric and Power Co.

VERNON "KOMAR" CRAIG

"Mr. Craig, who has an act featuring walking up knife-edged stairs, says he was recently informed that he holds the world record for lying on a bed of nails underneath a weight — 825 pounds."

— THE ASSOCIATED PRESS, IN A REPORT IN JULY 1971

ABOUT

- Born Jan. 7, 1932. Died March 7, 2010.
- Performed, beginning in 1963, as "Komar the Hindu Fakir" in 100 countries.
- As Komar, Craig slept on a bed of nails, walked on fire and climbed a ladder of knives.
- Owned the Guinness Book of World Records title for sleeping on a bed of nails until it was retired as too dangerous in the mid-1980s.
- Appeared on a number of NE Ohio and national television shows.

STARK CONNECTION

- Member of the Church of Jesus Christ of Latter Day Saints in Massillon.
- Worked as cheese maker and sales manager at Alpine Alpa near Wilmot.

LEVI LAMBORN

"Could I have something to show my friends? They'll never believe I spoke to you."

— REQUEST OF A 12-YEAR-OLD GIRL THAT CAUSED PRESIDENT WILLIAM MCKINLEY TO GIVE HER THE LAMBORN-INSPIRED RED CARNATION FROM HIS LAPEL ONLY SECONDS BEFORE HE WAS ASSASSINATED IN BUFFALO IN 1901.

ABOUT

- Born Oct. 10, 1829, Chester County, Pa. Died June 14, 1910.
- Doctor, horticulturist and politician who grew some of the first red carnations in the country.
- Lost to friend William McKinley in a bid in 1876 for a congressional seat.
- Before political debates, presented McKinley with a red carnation for his lapel, which McKinley adopted as a custom for his entire political career.
- Suggested that the scarlet carnation be designated the state flower.

STARK CONNECTION

- Set up a medical practice in Alliance.
- Founded the Alliance Ledger, the town's first newspaper.

THE REV. HAROLD HENNIGER

"In 1966, as he lay in the hospital after experiencing a heart attack, God laid it upon his heart to organize a Christian Hall of Fame. The Hall is housed at Canton Baptist Temple and ... (includes) men and women who have influenced the history of Christianity through the centuries."

— CHRISTIANHOF.ORG/HENNIGER

ABOUT

- Born May 4, 1924, Doylestown, Ohio. Died Oct. 25, 2004.
- Pastor emeritus, Canton Baptist Temple; served from 1947 to 1990.
- Credited with transforming Canton Baptist Temple into one of America's first "mega-churches," with a membership of 10,000.
- Built a 3,500-seat sanctuary at 515 Whipple Ave. NW in Perry Township in 1963.
- Introduced live TV broadcasts, Christian Hall of Fame.
- Offered prayer for an opening session of U.S. House of Representatives in 1976.

STARK CONNECTION

- Moved to Canton from Fort Worth in 1947.

RICHARD KINNEY

"A deaf-blind person is a walking, talking, living Sherlock Holmes most of his waking hours."

— FROM THE WRITINGS OF RICHARD KINNEY

ABOUT

- Born in 1924. Died in 1979.
- Educator, lecturer, author, poet, bowler, chess expert and world traveler.
- Blinded at 7 through illness and went deaf at 20.
- Third blind and deaf American to earn a university degree; second blind and deaf person, after Helen Keller, to earn a doctorate.
- Spoke in 40 countries and at many universities, while writing several textbooks on the education of the blind.

STARK CONNECTION

- Graduated as valedictorian of his high school class in East Sparta.
- Graduated summa cum laude and valedictorian from Mount Union College in 1955; earned doctorate from Mount Union in 1966.

JOSEPH J. CICCHETTI

"As he approached the casualties, he was struck in the head by a shell fragment, but with complete disregard for his gaping wound he continued to his comrades, lifted one and carried him on his shoulders 50 yards to safety. He then collapsed and died."

—MEDAL OF HONOR CITATION.

ABOUT

- Born June 8, 1923. Died Feb. 9, 1945.
- Private First Class, U.S. Army, Company A, 148th Infantry, 37th Infantry Division.
- Received Medal of Honor posthumously for rescuing wounded comrades during U.S. assault on Japanese forces in Manila, Philippines.
- Volunteered to organize a team that evacuated 14 wounded soldiers while exposed to machine gun, mortar and artillery fire.

STARK CONNECTION

- From Waynesburg.
- Buried in Sandy Valley Cemetery.

TED HENRY

"I hold a deep personal conviction that the mysteries of the spirit are the last, great journalistic frontier. We are constantly students at the feet of sages and teachers."

ABOUT

- Television news anchor whose career spanned more than 40 years in NE Ohio, most notably as the news anchor on Cleveland ABC affiliate WEWS Channel 5.
- Served as weeknight anchor for 34 years until his retirement in 2009.
- Traveled internationally to cover stories including the fall of the Berlin Wall and the death of Pope John Paul II.
- 1991 inductee into the Ohio Broadcasters Hall of Fame; 2007 inductee into the Ohio Associated Press Broadcasters Hall of Fame.

STARK CONNECTION

- Born in 1946 in Canton.
- Graduated from Canton Central Catholic High School.
- Began college at Walsh University before graduating from Kent State University.

JAMES DUNCAN

"He was the most unselfish man we ever knew. He sought money as a means, not as an end. Liberal and generous to a fault, he never knew its value except as it enabled him to be generous."

— FROM DUNCAN'S OBITUARY IN THE REPOSITORY, APRIL 1, 1863

ABOUT

- Born May 2, 1789. Died March 15, 1863.
- Founded the City of Massillon in 1826.
- His wife, Eliza, named the town after French Bishop Jean-Baptiste Massillon.

STARK CONNECTION

- Built and lived in house that is now home of the Massillon Public Library.
- Donated money to help build St. Timothy's Episcopal Church.
- President of Massillon Rolling Mill and Bank of Massillon.
- Came to the area in 1816, originally settling on land that would be Massillon.

LEE KESSLER

"At that moment I could only think that everyone has the right to die with dignity and there was this poor soul who died with such obscurity."

— KESSLER, DESCRIBING A SCENE FROM A GERMAN CONCENTRATION CAMP WHEN HE WAS A POW DURING WWII

ABOUT

- Born May 25, 1921 and died Oct. 3, 2003.
- Joined the Army Air Corps with the onset of World War II. Trained to be a gunner, flew 18 missions in the European Theater of Operations before being shot down over Germany in May 1943. Witnessed atrocities in Nazi Germany.
- German POW until liberated by the U.S. Army.
- Created artwork inspired by his World War II experiences, including "The Hand." The rendering is based on the dead body of a man who had been a prisoner at a German concentration camp.

STARK CONNECTION

- Returned to his hometown of Canton following World War II.

KEN CAZAN

"If you love to sing, enjoy it. Don't think 'I'm going to go into opera' necessarily. But don't be afraid to go to a school and take voice lessons also. Ease your way into it."

ABOUT

- Chairs the vocal arts and opera division at the University of Southern California Thornton School of Music, where he also is resident stage director.
- Has directed more than 150 plays, operas and musicals in North America and Europe.
- Helped write libretto for new opera "Frau Schindler."
- Has served as guest stage director at Juilliard School, Academy of Vocal Arts, Curtis Institute of Music, Indiana University and Manhattan School of Music.

STARK CONNECTION

- Attended Kent State University at Stark from 1975 to 1977 and has been recognized as an outstanding alumnus.
- Has worked with students at Stark County high schools on theater projects.

JOE R. HASTINGS

"As spearhead of the 3d Platoon's attack, he advanced, firing his gun held at hip height, disregarding the bullets that whipped past him, until the assault had carried 175 yards to the objective. In this charge he and the riflemen he led killed or wounded many of the fanatical enemy and put two machine guns out of action."

— EXCERPT FROM MEDAL OF HONOR CITATION

ABOUT
- Born April 8, 1925. Died April 16, 1945.
- Private first class, U.S. Army, Company C, 386th Infantry, 97th Infantry Division
- Received Medal of Honor for leading attacks in the face of German fire at Drabenderhohe on April 12, 1945.
- Squad leader of a light machine-gun section. His attack allowed his unit to regroup and evacuate wounded.
- Killed in action four days later.

STARK CONNECTION
- Graduate of Magnolia High School, formerly of Chicago.
- Buried in Magnolia Cemetery.

JOHN FAWCETT

"John Fawcett was a man who never sought honors for himself. What distinction came to him was merited. Drafted for service on the school board, he received the highest vote. That in itself is an expression of the community's high regard for a man who devoted his life to his family and his community. His death is a great personal loss to me."

— WILLIAM G. SAXTON, PRESIDENT OF FIRST NATIONAL BANK

ABOUT
- Born in 1890 in Canton and was a member of one of the city's prominent families. Died Oct. 23, 1935, from pneumonia.
- President of First Trust and Savings Bank, and previously served as general manager of The Federal Garment Co.

STARK CONNECTION
- Member of Canton City Schools' Board of Education from 1932-35.
- "Endowed with a never-say-die spirit," he became one of Central High School's finest basketball players.
- Was known for his philanthropic gifts and for serving on committees and campaigns to help those in need.
- Namesake of former Fawcett Stadium, which opened in 1939.

HIRAM A. DELAVIE

ABOUT

- Entered Union Army as a private, left as a 1st Sergeant.
- Wounded at Second Battle of Bull Run during Civil War in 1862.
- Was awarded Congressional Medal of Honor for bravery, the nation's highest award during combat, for capturing Confederate flag at Battle of Five Forks in Virginia on April 1, 1865.

- Buried in St. Peters Cemetery, Pittsburgh.

STARK CONNECTION

- Born in 1824 in Stark County. Died in 1902.
- Sergeant from Stark County in 11th Pennsylvania Infantry.

WILLIAM ARCHINAL

"Gallantry in the charge of the 'volunteer storming party.'"

— CITATION ON MEDAL OF HONOR, WHICH WAS ISSUED JUNE 10, 1894

ABOUT

- Born in Germany on June 3, 1840. Died May 10, 1919.
- Emigrated to the U.S. in 1860 and settled in Canal Dover, Ohio.
- In August 1861, enlisted in Company I, 30th Ohio Infantry of the Union Army.
- Awarded the Medal of Honor in 1894 for role in 1863 attack on Vicksburg, Miss. He volunteered to be part of a unit that rushed at the enemy's fortifications holding logs amid open fire from Confederate troops in an attempt to build a bridge.

- Participated in many battles, including at Antietam and the second Bull Run.

STARK CONNECTION

- After the Civil War, he got a job in Massillon. Moved to Canton in 1868.
- Appointed postmaster general in 1886 by President Grover Cleveland.
- Became Canton City Council member and member of Board of Education.

56

JOSEPH DAVENPORT

"The Fremont Mill bridge is an excellent example of the work of Joseph Davenport's Massillon Iron Bridge Co., a major bridge fabricator who erected many of these type of bridges throughout the nation. This bridge is also of great interest because it employs the unusual built-up lattice girders of Davenport's patent."

— GEOFFREY GOLDBERG, ENGINEER, NATIONAL PARK SERVICE, U.S. DEPARTMENT OF THE INTERIOR

ABOUT
- Entrepreneur and builder who, with his brother, built the first American-style railway coaches with an aisle down the middle in 1832.
- Inventor of the cowcatcher in 1840 and snow plow for locomotives.
- Creator of an early steam car, a forerunner of the electric trolley.
- Designed and built steel truss bridges across the nation.

STARK CONNECTION
- Born in 1815, moved to Massillon in the 1850s.
- Founded Massillon Iron Bridge Co. in 1869, incorporated in 1887.
- Built Oak Knoll Park Bridge in Massillon in 1859.
- Patented his bridge designs.
- Died at the age of 97.

JOSEPH E. FISHER

"There is only one way to treat a customer… so that they come back again and again."

ABOUT
- Came to Canton from Baltimore in 1903.
- Served in World War I.
- Made cigars at his father's store, obtained a law degree and then went into business with his father at a clothing store on Dueber Avenue.
- After business slowed during the Great Depression, he opened Fisher's Super Market in 1933 on Navarre Road and Garfield Avenue SW.

STARK CONNECTION
- A Central High School graduate.
- Founded the local grocery store, which has remained in the Fisher family for generations. The grocers' seven locations employ more than 700 people in Stark County.

JOHN E. CARNAHAN

"Until he was stricken ill, Carnahan was active in the business world, and despite his advanced age, made frequent trips to inspect his oil fields and land holdings in the southwest."

— OBITUARY FOR CARNAHAN

ABOUT

- Born Aug. 10, 1849, in Leechburg, Pa. Died July 2, 1936, in Canton.
- Leased 8,000 acres in Armstrong County, Pa., and opened what was believed to be the greatest gas field in Pennsylvania, becoming a millionaire from oil leases.
- Owned steel plant in Norwalk, Ohio, and an oil refinery in Kentucky as well as a banana plantation in Mexico and farmland in Arkansas.

STARK CONNECTION

- Built a rolling mill in Canton in 1897; he sold the mill, which eventually was purchased by U.S. Steel, in 1901.
- Built a tin plate mill in Canton and established the Carnahan Land.

RAYMOND G. DRAGE

"He was the one who formulated vocational education and brought it to Stark County. But it just wasn't his name on the building, he lived it."

— RICHARD FAIELLO, FORMER VOCATIONAL DIRECTOR OF R.G. DRAGE CAREER TECHNICAL CENTER

ABOUT

- Born Aug. 22, 1916. Died Dec. 12, 2006.
- Spent roughly 40 years in education and is credited with introducing the concept of sharing resources regionally to other county school systems in Ohio.
- Served with the U.S. Army's 795th Anti-aircraft Artillery during World War II.
- He earned four battle stars and was awarded the Jubilee of Liberty Medal.

STARK CONNECTION

- Graduated from Navarre High School in 1934.
- Served 17 years as superintendent of the Stark County Schools District. Also worked for Plain Local School District, Robertsville School in Paris Township and Pigeon Run School in Tuscarawas Township during his career.
- Namesake of the R.G. Drage Career Technical Center in Massillon.

DAN OBROVAC

"He got up there quickly, and I wasn't paying attention. Like they say, 'you snooze, you lose.'"

— KAREEM ABDUL-JABBAR (FORMERLY LEW ALCINDOR), TALKING ABOUT THE 1967 OPENING JUMP TO THE DAYTON DAILY NEWS IN 2011.

ABOUT
- Born June 23, 1947, in Canton. Died April 21, 2010.
- Starred in basketball at the University of Dayton as a 6-foot-10 center.
- Won the opening tip in the 1967 NCAA Tournament Championship game against UCLA over All-American Lew Alcindor — it is believed to be the only jump Alcindor lost during his remarkable college career. UCLA, though, won the game, 79-64, to start the Bruins on a streak of seven straight titles under John Wooden.
- A photo of the tip at Freedom Hall in Louisville, Ky., became famous once Sports Illustrated picked it up. It still hangs inside the concourse of UD Arena.

STARK CONNECTION
- 1965 graduate of Central Catholic High School, where he averaged 24.3 points per game as a senior for the 14-2 Crusaders.

PARALEE COMPTON

"The years have gone by really quickly. They've been rewarding. It is with bittersweetness that I leave because there are so many things that need to be done. But, now is the time."

ABOUT
- Born May 9, 1931, Madison County, Ala.; came to Canton at age 4.
- Married Daniel Mordecai Compton. Mother of three — Marian Yvonne Compton, Madeline Annette Harris and Andrea Beth Hudson.

STARK CONNECTION
- Compton served in many leadership and administrative roles with the Canton City Schools for nearly 50 years. She was the first female and the first African American to serve as the assistant superintendent of Canton City Schools.
- Lathrop Elementary School was renamed in honor of Paralee Watkins Compton Oct. 16, 2004.
- Compton retired in 1993. In 2000, she came out of retirement to coordinate GEAR UP, a college preparatory program beginning with Canton City middle school students, taking them on through high school and getting them ready for college.

JACOB S. COXEY SR.

"We will send a petition to Washington with boots on."

ABOUT

- Born April 16, 1854, in Sellingrove, Pa. Died May 18, 1951, in Massillon
- During the Panic of 1893, he led a group of unemployed workers in a march on Washington, hoping to persuade the government to create jobs by initiating public works projects.
- Coxey's Army left Massillon on March 30, 1894, and reached Washington on April 30. The next day, Coxey and others were arrested for walking on the grass outside the Capitol.
- Elected mayor of Massillon in 1931 and served one two-year term.
- Ran for public office more than a dozen times, winning only the Massillon mayor's race in 1931. Also ran for U.S. representative, U.S. senator, Ohio governor and president as a member of the Greenback, People's, Republican, Democratic, Interracial Independent Political and United States Farmer-Labor parties, and as an independent.

STARK CONNECTION

- Moved to Massillon in 1881 and opened a sand quarry called Coxey Silica Sand Co.

JOSHUA JAY

"Magic should cause people to reconsider what they think they know and the way they perceive things."

ABOUT

- As a close-up magician and magic lecturer, Jay has appeared in more than 50 countries, and on "The Today Show" and "Good Morning America."
- At age 17, Jay was crowned champion at the World Magic Seminar, and in 2012 was named Magician of the Year by the Society of American Magicians.
- Jay has written many how-to books about magic, including "Magic: The Complete Course" and "Big Magic For Little Hands."

STARK CONNECTION

- Born Oct. 30, 1981, in Canton.
- Graduated from GlenOak High School in 2000.

DELORIS M. COPE

"I really appreciate the recognition this has given the various projects I am involved in. It is really quite an honor to be part of the women who work so hard in this community."

ABOUT
- Born in Canton on May 21, 1929. Died June 25, 1998.
- Graduated from Lincoln High School and Canton Actual Business College; attended Mount Union College and Kent State University.
- Ran for Canton City Council president in 1985.

STARK CONNECTION
- Tireless volunteer for many organizations, including United Way, Girl Scouts, 4-H, Canton YWCA and Salvation Army; active with Stark County Hunger Task Force, Canton Symphony, Civic Opera and Council of Churches; received United Way Gold Key Award and was 1982 Junior League Woman of the Year.

ROBERT KING

"His outstanding leadership and countless hours of meetings and door-to-door campaigning made possible the construction of the present Alliance High School building."

— ALLIANCE HIGH SCHOOL ALUMNI FOUNDATION

ABOUT
- Worked as chief of surgery at Alliance City Hospital from 1962-75.
- Was the team physician for Alliance High School and what is now the University of Mount Union.
- Earned his medical degree from Harvard Medical School in 1937.
- Died in 2001 at age 89.

STARK CONNECTION
- Graduated from Alliance High School in 1929 and Mount Union in 1933.
- Chaired the "Alliance High School Now" committee, which was credited with raising the money needed to build a new high school.

DON NEHLEN

"I used to sneak into Fawcett Stadium because I didn't have any money to pay to get in. I ended up coaching there."

ABOUT
- Played quarterback at Bowling Green from 1955-57.
- Compiled a 202-128-8 record as the head football coach at Bowling Green (1968-76) and West Virginia (1980-2000).
- Hired as Canton South's head football coach as a 23-year-old in 1959, going 22-14-2 in four seasons. The Wildcats went 9-1 in 1962, setting a school single-season wins record that still stands.
- Went 9-1 with McKinley High in 1964, falling to Massillon 20-14 in the season finale to finish second behind the Tigers in the Ohio Associated Press poll.

STARK CONNECTION
- Grew up on Broad Avenue in Canton and starred in multiple sports at Lincoln High. He quarterbacked Lincoln to city title in 1953 while gaining all-city and all-county honors.

MARY O. McLAIN HARRISON

"As I have been given a lift by others, so I hope others can be given a lift by something I do or say."

— IN AN OCT. 13, 1957 REPOSITORY PROFILE

ABOUT
- Born in Harrisburg, Va., in 1878. Died May 15, 1967.
- In 1924, instrumental in founding of Canton Quota Club. Served in every office, received highest honor in 1957.
- Helped lead efforts to sell Liberty Bonds during World War I.
- In 1943, founded the Russian War Relief and Greek War Relief organizations in Canton as part of effort to help out during WWII.
- Studied at University of Pittsburgh while her daughter was a college student; earned a degree in "teaching foreign born children" and taught beginning English at McKinley High School night school.

STARK CONNECTION
- Moved to Canton at a young age.

PHILIP C. FLEISCHER

"My father probably had more perseverance than anyone I know. When he put his mind toward something, it was done."

— FRANK FLEISCHER

ABOUT
▪ Born in Thomasville, Ga. Came to Canton in 1920.

STARK CONNECTION
▪ Negotiated with the Junior League of Canton for a home for the blind. The first Philomathcon Society was at 716 Cleveland Ave. SW. The league donated it, but the society had to pay off the $3,300 mortgage and the $1,900 in back taxes. Within 10 days, Fleischer obtained the cash in donations. He also obtained 10 beds donated by the Hollanden Hotel in Cleveland.
▪ Founder of Fleischer Shoe Co. in Middletown. Opened the Canton Fleischer Shoe in 1920. It was a general family shoe store, specializing in orthopedic shoes.
▪ President of the Downtown Merchants Association.

TOM WEISKOPF

"My problem was that I wanted to play perfectly. Nobody can be perfect. If I shot 66 or 65 but played sloppily, it didn't mean much. I wanted to hit the required shot every time. I couldn't stand mediocrity."

— WEISKOPF INTERVIEW WITH GOLF MAGAZINE, 2014

ABOUT
▪ Won 16 PGA Tour titles from 1968-1982, including seven in 1973, when he won the British Open. He also finished runner-up at the Masters four times (1969, 1972, 1974, 1975) and was second at the U.S. Open in 1976. Won the U.S. Senior Open in 1995.
▪ Has designed more than 40 golf courses around the world.
▪ Nicknamed "The Towering Inferno" for his height (6-foot-3) and his temper on the course.

STARK CONNECTION
▪ Born Nov. 9, 1942, in Massillon.
▪ His mother, Eva, taught herself to play golf at Massillon's Elmwood Country Club (now The Elms) and later finished second to Patty Berg at the 1938 U.S. Women's Open.

CHARLES M. RUSSELL

ABOUT

- Came to Massillon from New England in 1838 for business related to the canal that passed through Massillon.
- Russell brothers founded C.M. Russell & Co. in 1842. Company built threshers and other agricultural equipment, then train cars, then steam engines in 1864.
- Became one of the largest builders of steam engines in the industry, building its famous steam traction engines.

STARK CONNECTION

- Biggest employer in Massillon for much of the mid-1800s.
- Died at age 67 from apoplexy in February 1860. His brothers continued to lead his company.

FIG. 248.   COMPOUND TRACTION ENGINE.   THE RUSSELL CO.

MABEL HARTZELL

"She has quite a long resume. You can pretty much name a club in town, you will find she was on the founding list. We still occasionally have people come through the house that say they had Mabel in school. They say she was tough but fair. She made an impact on people that she taught. She was quite a lady."

— MICHELLE DILLON, PRESIDENT OF THE ALLIANCE HISTORICAL SOCIETY

ABOUT

- Born Jan. 1, 1875, in Saginaw, Mich. Died Dec. 2, 1954, in Alliance.
- Obtained bachelor's degree from Mount Union College and master's degree from Ohio State University.
- Founded the Alliance chapter of the American Red Cross.
- Founded Alliance Woman's Club.

STARK CONNECTION

- The Mabel Hartzell Historical Club at 840 N. Park Ave. was her home, which she bequeathed to the Alliance Historical Society.
- Taught at Alliance High School for 30 years.

JAMES R. FINDLAY

"May you enjoy fair winds and following seas."

— WORDS EXPRESSED IN HIS OBITUARY

ABOUT

- Born July 23, 1938, in Mason City, Iowa.
- Entered Naval Aviation Officer Candidate School in June 1960, earning his Wings of Gold in November 1961.
- Flew in the JFK funeral procession.
- Became one of the first ensigns assigned to fly the F-4 Phantom and was one of the first Top Gun pilots, flying in 206 combat missions.

STARK CONNECTION

- Chosen as one of 200 inductees for the Greatest Sons and Daughters for the Stark County Wall of Fame 2003 on behalf of the Ohio Bicentennial Celebration.
- Died May 31, 2003. Buried in Canton's North Lawn Cemetery.

THE REV. PETER HERBRUCK

"As I look back upon my past life, I see everywhere the wonderful guidance of God. I see how all the events of my life hang together like the links of a chain."

ABOUT

- Born Feb. 8, 1813, Grossteinhausen, Germany. Died Sept. 23, 1895.

STARK CONNECTION

- One of Stark County's longest-serving clergymen, serving at German Reformed Church of Canton from 1832 to 1886.
- First resident pastor of St. Jacob's Reformed Church in Plain Township, 1845.
- Father of 10 children; one son, the Rev. Emil Herbruck, served Trinity Reformed Church for 51 years.

DICK KEMPTHORN

"I was at the right place at the right time so many times during my life. Some people are lucky."

ABOUT

- Played fullback and linebacker at Michigan from 1947-49, going 25-2-1 while helping the Wolverines win national titles in 1947 and 1948.
- Was drafted by the Philadelphia Eagles in the 14th round of the 1948 NFL draft and by the Cleveland Browns in the second round of the 1949 AAFC draft, but bypassed pro football to return to Canton to work at his father's car dealership, which expanded to the Kempthorn Auto Mall under his leadership.
- Enlisted in the Naval Reserve after high school and spent 18 months at sea during World War II, much of it in the Pacific Theater.

STARK CONNECTION

- Born Oct. 23, 1926, in Canton.
- Two-year starter at quarterback and linebacker at McKinley High, helping the Bulldogs go 16-2-2 and win a state title in 1942.

THE REV. WARREN CHAVERS

"I think I am like most black people of my generation who were teenagers during the Malcolm X and Martin Luther King Jr. years. But if all I can do is trace myself back to a black man who was assassinated, then I'm in trouble."

ABOUT

- Born April 22, 1952.
- Founder/Senior Pastor (1979–2013) at Deliverance Christian Church.
- Pastor emeritus status – August 2013.
- Wife, Adrienne; nine children, 27 grandchildren, two great-grandchildren.

STARK CONNECTION

- 1970 graduate of Timken High School; attended Kent State University and Moody Bible College; graduated from Bethany Bible College with a sacred literature degree in 1984.
- Founder and president of Deliverance Bible Institute, 1987 to present.
- Co-founder, Stark County Black Federation.

HAROLD G. EPPERSON

"Determined to save his comrades, Pfc. Epperson unhesitatingly chose to sacrifice himself and, diving upon the deadly missile, absorbed the shattering violence of the exploding charge in his own body."

— MEDAL OF HONOR CITATION

ABOUT

- Born July 14, 1923, in Akron. Served in the U.S. Marines during World War II.
- On June 25, 1944, in Saipan in the Northern Mariana Islands, Epperson hurled himself onto a Japanese grenade, saving his fellow Marines. He died at age 20.
- Awarded the Medal of Honor posthumously.
- A Navy destroyer launched Dec. 23, 1945, was named for him.

STARK CONNECTION

- Grew up in Massillon and graduated from Washington High School in 1943.
- About 8,500 people attended the medal ceremony at Tiger Stadium, where his mother, Jonett B. Epperson of Mt. Sterling, Ky., received the medal.

WILLIAM R. "TIM" TIMKEN

"At the company, everything is accomplished by a team. But in swimming, it's you and you alone. Money doesn't matter. Your name doesn't matter. Your success is accomplished on your own and depends upon how much effort you put into it as an individual."

— FROM HIS GOLD MEDALLION ENTRY ON THE INTERNATIONAL SWIMMING HALL OF FAME WEBSITE.

ABOUT

- Born 1938 in Canton.
- Joined Timken Co. in 1962 after graduating from Stanford University.
- Served as company director from 1965 to 2005.
- Named chairman in 1975; also served as chief executive officer and president.
- Appointed in 2005 by President George W. Bush as U.S. Ambassador to Germany. Served until December 2008.
- In 2009, received the International Swimming Hall of Fame Gold Medallion Award, which is presented each year to recognize significant achievements of a former competitive swimmer.
- Served as director for Diebold, Trinova Corp., Louisiana Land and Exploration Co., and Texas Energy, as well as the Pro Football Hall of Fame.

STARK CONNECTION

- Stark County native and resident.
- Led the Timken Co. and Timken Foundation.

PETE ELLIOTT

"Those who met Pete and knew him, they could never say a bad word about him. He was not only a great football player, he was a great athlete and a great gentleman."

— CANTON BUSINESSMAN DICK KEMPTHORN, ELLIOTT'S MICHIGAN TEAMMATE ON THE 1947-48 TEAMS.

ABOUT

▪ From 1945-48, he became the first athlete in University of Michigan history to earn 12 letters (football, basketball and golf).
▪ Quarterbacked the Wolverines to undefeated records and national titles in 1947 and 1948.
▪ Head football coach at Nebraska (1956), Cal (1957-59), Illinois (1960-66) and Miami, Fla. (1973-74). Led the Illini to a Big Ten title and Rose Bowl victory in 1963.

STARK CONNECTION

▪ Served as the Pro Football Hall of Fame's executive director from 1979-1995.
▪ Sat on the Hall's board of directors until he died in 2013 at age 86.

MIKE HERSHBERGER

"I remember how true he was to himself and everyone he met. He was a man's man, a guy's guy and he had a faith that was unshakable. He went to church religiously and he was a big influence in my life. He was a great representative for Massillon."

— TOM MELDRUM, CHILDHOOD FRIEND, AFTER HERSHBERGER'S DEATH IN 2012.

ABOUT

▪ Played 11 seasons as an outfielder in the major leagues with the Chicago White Sox (1961-64 and 1971), Kansas City/Oakland Athletics (1965-69) and Milwaukee Brewers (1970). Batted .252 with 900 career hits, including 26 homers. Blessed with a powerful arm, he led the American League in outfield assists in 1965 (14) and 1967 (17).

STARK CONNECTION

▪ Born Oct. 9, 1939, in Massillon. Died July 1, 2012, in Massillon.
▪ Two-sport standout at Massillon High, earning All-Ohio honors as a tailback while also playing outfielder and a pitcher on the baseball team.
▪ Inducted into the Massillon High "Wall of Champions" in 1994.

JOHN DANNER

"These cases, with their immense load, revolve with a slight touch of the hand, are noiseless in operation, and will last a lifetime."

— FROM A "DANNER CATALOG"

ABOUT
- Born March 10, 1823 and died April 12, 1918.
- Gunsmith, merchant and inventor of the "pivot and post" revolving bookcase.
- Founded the John Danner Manufacturing Co. in Canton in 1874.
- Danner's bookcase appeared in the 1894 Montgomery Ward's catalog.
- His bookcase won a gold medal at the Paris International Exhibition in 1878.
- Danner Manufacturing burned in 1903, was rebuilt on the same foundation, and Danner sold it when he was 93.

STARK CONNECTION
- Danner was born in Canton and died in the city at 95.
- Canton city council member, board of education member, and historian who wrote "Old Landmarks of Canton and Stark County, Ohio."

LOUELLA BUKER

"A guiding force and a shining example for others."

— EXCERPT FROM "STARK COUNTY WALL OF FAME: OUR GREATEST SONS AND DAUGHTERS"

ABOUT
- Born in 1899. Died in 1982.
- Organized and created the Stark County Republican Women in the 1920s.
- Helped found the Stark County Tuberculosis Association, now called the American Lung Association of Stark-Wayne.
- Served as director of the Family Service Society and Children's Bureau, the Phillis Wheatley Association and the Great Trail Council of the Girl Scouts.
- Participated in Walsh and Malone college advisory boards, the Mental Health Association and the Canton Players Guild Theatre.

STARK CONNECTION
- First woman on the Stark County Board of Elections.
- First woman to serve as foreman of the Stark County grand jury.
- First woman to lead the Stark County Republican Party.

JIM BALLARD

"I have always said the best thing about football is the relationships I had with the guys at Mount Union."

ABOUT

▪ Set 17 Division III passing records over his three-year career while quarterbacking Mount Union to its first national title in 1993. Also won the Gagliardi Trophy that season, given to the top player in Division III.

▪ Played 13 seasons of professional football over a 10-year span, mostly in the World League/NFL Europe, the Canadian Football League and the Arena Football League. Although he never appeared in a NFL game, he had stints with the Cincinnati Bengals and Buffalo Bills.

▪ Inducted into the College Football Hall of Fame in 2008.

STARK CONNECTION

▪ A Cuyahoga Falls native, Ballard graduated from Mount Union in 1994 and still lives in Canton, where he runs the Jim Ballard Quarterback Academy.

JACK HAZEN

"I'm very happy to have spent my career at Malone. I've got friends who say I'm either very loyal or very stupid for staying. But I really believe in what Malone stands for."

ABOUT

▪ Over his 50-year head coaching career, he helped Malone's men's cross country team win national titles in 1972, 2007, 2008 and 2009 and led the women to the 1999 title.

▪ Malone's men's cross country team is the winningest program in NAIA history, finishing in the top 10 36 times. He has coached more than 325 NAIA All-Americans in track and cross country.

▪ Served as an assistant coach for the USA Track and Field team during the 2012 Olympic Games. Also serves on the USA Track and Field board of directors.

STARK CONNECTION

▪ Grew up near Alliance and graduated from Marlboro High in 1958.

NATE TORRENCE

"I wasn't much of a basketball player … but I could make people laugh."

ABOUT
- Voiced Benjamin Clawhauser, the cheetah cop, in the 2016 animated movie "Zootopia."
- Performed in Capital One commercials with David Spade.
- Had roles in movies "Get Smart" and "She's Out of My League."
- Played Allison Janney's son in the 2011 TV series "Mr. Sunshine."
- Starred in the six-episode run of "Weird Loners."
- Has played spot roles in TV shows such as "CSI" and "How I Met Your Mother."
- Studied improv with Second City Players Workshop in Chicago.

STARK CONNECTION
- Born in Canton.
- Performed in theater productions in Canton following graduation.

JIM BURNETT

"People have a right to know, and we have a right to broadcast."

ABOUT
- Born 1925. Died July 6, 1998.
- Award-winning announcer and news director at WHBC Radio from 1953 to 1988.
- Before joining WHBC, worked at WICA in Ashtabula, WFAH in Alliance, WFMJ in Youngstown.
- Honored by Cleveland Press Club, Society of Professional Journalists, Associated Press, the Radio and Television News Directors Association, Canton Professional Educators' Association.
- 1992 inductee, Broadcasters Hall of Fame.
- Served on the boards of the Ohio Associated Press Broadcasters, Red Cross Canton chapter, Canton Urban League and the Stark County Drug and Alcohol Addiction Services. Chairman, Heart Association drive.
- Resident of North Canton.

71

FRANK C. BEANE

"As bad as America is, it's always the Americans that'll come along and make something right."

ABOUT
- Born, March 25, 1902, Oklahoma Territory. Died Dec. 31, 2001.
- A familiar figure in downtown Canton, Beane was the city's first black attorney.
- Graduate, Wilberforce University, Ohio State University School of Law; passed the bar exam in 1939, while working as a janitor for the Ohio Highway Department.
- World War II Army Air Corps volunteer.

- In 1943, resumed private practice with future judge Clay Hunter; special assistant to Ohio Attorneys General Paul Brown, William Saxbe and Hugh Jenkins.

STARK CONNECTION
- Moved to Canton in 1923.
- Member board of trustees, Central State University.

RABBI PAUL GORIN

"It's been an interesting life."

ABOUT
- Born March 25, 1911, Buffalo, N.Y. Died Oct. 29, 1996.
- Rabbi emeritus Temple Israel, Canton, serving from 1954 to 1980. Previously served in Chicago and St. Louis.
- Served in World War II as the chief Jewish chaplain for Gen. George Patton's Third Army, and with the United Kingdom Base, London; regimental chaplain, 78th Lightning Division.
- One of the first Jewish chaplains to enter the Dachau concentration camp after its liberation.
- Assisted displaced persons in Germany and Bavaria. Official observer, Nuremberg trials.

- Recipient of the Bronze Star.
- Honorary chaplain, Canton Police Department; social action chair, Canton Ministerial Association; attended the historic March on Washington; chaplain, Canton chapter of Jewish War Veterans.
- Canton Chamber of Commerce Man of the Year; Canton Rotary Club Paul Harris Fellow; Jewish Community Federation Kopstein Community Award; Walsh College lecturer.

STARK CONNECTION
- Moved to Canton in 1954.

LOY JOSEPH "JOE" YODER

"My mentor, my employer, my guide. He was just regarded as a fountain of knowledge."

— FORMER COUNTY AUDITOR WILLIAM B. BOWMAN

ABOUT

- Born June 12, 1902; died October 1989.
- Attended Hickory College district school and the township high school at Harrisburg.
- Elected to eight consecutive terms, serving 32 years, as Stark County auditor.
- Served term as president of Ohio Auditors Association.
- First county officeholder to computerize operations in 1970.
- Supported a public school in Thailand, where his son was a missionary.

STARK CONNECTION

- Born on his family's Nimishillen Township farm.
- Owned Yoder-Gillette Tire Co.

GEORGE V. KELLEY

"The President of the United States of America, in the name of Congress, takes pleasure in presenting the Medal of Honor to Captain (Infantry) George V. Kelley, United States Army, for extraordinary heroism on 30 November 1864, while serving with Company A, 104th Ohio Infantry, in action at Franklin, Tennessee, for capture of flag supposed to be of Cheatham's Corps (Confederate States of America)."

— FROM KELLY'S MEDAL OF HONOR AWARD

ABOUT

- Enlisted in the 104th Ohio Infantry in Massillon on July 30, 1862.
- In 1864, promoted to captain and commander of Company A.
- In November 1864, during the Battle of Franklin (Tennessee), captured a Confederate flag. He was awarded a Congressional Medal of Honor in February 1865 for his gallantry.
- After the war, he returned to Ohio and married Fannie Bliss in October 1866. She died and he moved to Colorado to become a rancher, remarrying in 1890.
- Died in Denver on Nov. 4, 1905, at age 62.

STARK CONNECTION

- Born on March 23, 1843, in Massillon.

LEONARD E. SHULL

"Shull attended country school and became a clerk in the hardware store of Moses, Couch & Strayer at a salary of $50 a year. He boarded with the proprietors' families and slept in the store."

— FROM SHULL'S OBITUARY

ABOUT

- Born April 23, 1865; died in 1945.
- Organized Shull Steel Casting Co. (later named Canton Steel Foundry).
- Active in Local 431 McKinley Lodge, F. & A.M.
- Officer in Washington Council, Jr. O.U.A.M.
- 50-year member of the Masonic Order.
- Secretary-treasurer of Willowdale Country Club.

STARK CONNECTION

- Born on a Stark County farm and attended a country school.
- Masonic delegate to the funeral of President William McKinley.

STEVE LUKE

"I was very fortunate and blessed to have played for Massillon and to have grown up in Massillon, and very fortunate to have played for Coach (Bob) Commings. He taught us to believe in ourselves and how to win."

ABOUT

- Started at center and cornerback at Ohio State, playing in three straight Rose Bowls and helping the Buckeyes win three straight Big Ten titles.
- Drafted in the fourth round by the Green Bay Packers in 1975 and played in every game (with 75 starts) at safety over the next six seasons.
- Became a player agent, representing 23 players at his peak. Was Massillon standout Chris Spielman's first agent.

STARK CONNECTION

- Born Sept. 4, 1953, in Massillon.
- Played center, tight end and linebacker for the Tigers in 1969-70, earning third team All-Ohio honors while co-captaining the undefeated 1970 team that won the school's last state poll title. Member of the school's "Wall of Champions."

JAMES BRIDGES

"Our mission is to help children and families affected by neglect, abuse, and abandonment realize their worth and achieve the possibilities of their lives."

— PATHWAY MISSION STATEMENT

ABOUT

- Born March 11, 1944, in Ashland, Ky.; died Nov. 16, 2009, in North Canton.
- Educated at Malone, Michigan State and Case Western Reserve universities.
- Worked at Stark County Child Welfare Department, now called Department of Human Services.
- Founded Pathway Caring for Children in 1973, then named Stark County Group Home.
- Known for his constant caring and unceasing service to others in his community.

STARK CONNECTION

- Worked with an inner-city ministry in Canton that was helping the poor.
- Longtime director of Pathway Caring for Children.

SHIRLEY GIVENS

"It's written for the child. Most methods are written for the teacher."

— SHIRLEY GIVENS, ABOUT HER VIOLIN INSTRUCTION BOOK, "ADVENTURES IN VIOLINLAND"

ABOUT

- Born in 1931 in Louisville.
- Graduate of Juilliard School of Music.
- Actress and violinist who won eight national competitions.
- At age 5 was one of 20 contestants chosen from 27,000 entrants for "Search for Talent" in California.
- Debuted in violin performances at 11 and played recitals throughout the country.
- Played a command performance for President Dwight D. Eisenhower.
- Composer, author and teacher at Peabody Conservatory (emeritus), Juilliard (precollege), and Mannes College.
- Originator of the Shirley Givens Method for Teaching.

STARK CONNECTION

- Returned in 2009 for a violin performance in Louisville in celebration of the Stark County bicentennial.

JUDGE IRA G. TURPIN

"I never forgot what my grandfather said to me. He said, 'Now, son, whatever you want to be, you try to be the best.'"

ABOUT

- Born March 26, 1925, in Canton; died Aug. 11, 1989.
- Served in the U.S. Army from 1943 to 1946.
- Appointed Stark County's first black chief assistant prosecutor.
- Elected Common Pleas Court judge in 1972, serving until 1983.
- Elected to Fifth District Court of Appeals, serving from 1983 until retirement in 1989.

STARK CONNECTION

- Graduated from McKinley High School.
- Earned law degree at William McKinley School of Law.

MARY MARTIN

"You had to ask her for books. No one — not even grown-ups — was allowed to go to the shelves except Miss Martin herself."

— FROM A HISTORY OF THE EARLY YEARS OF STARK COUNTY DISTRICT LIBRARY.

ABOUT

- Born in Bucyrus in 1851; died in 1928.
- First librarian of Canton Public Library, serving 38 years.
- Martin's salary was $400 per year when she became librarian in 1885.
- Charter member of Canton Woman's Club.
- Active in the Chamber of Commerce, YWCA, DAR and Quota Club.
- Member of the Presbyterian church.

STARK CONNECTION

- Daughter of Henry S. Martin, a superintendent of Canton City Schools.
- Beloved in the Canton community.

OLGA ERZIGKEIT

"The answer to what we can do about our deepest needs is to be found within us... not in the world somewhere else ... not in the lives of others ... but within us and projection of ourselves beyond ourselves."

— 1959 SPEECH "GOOD CITIZENSHIP: HOW TO ATTAIN IT"

ABOUT

- Born May 28, 1910, in Canton; died March 4, 2002, at age 91.
- Won public speaking and writing contests by the Freedoms Foundation at Valley Forge, including eight George Washington Honor Medals. Used prize money to fund local essay contests.
- Three-time president of the Mercy Alumni Association.
- In 1956, honored as Woman of the Year by the Ohio State Federation of Business and Professional Women's Clubs.
- A registered nurse who worked in the occupational health field at area companies.

STARK CONNECTION

- 1928 graduate of McKinley High School; 1933 graduate of the Mercy Hospital School of Nursing.

FRANKLIN CARR

"We traced Franklin Carr over three states ... then he went out to the Indian Territory. Nothing after that. Don't know where he's buried ... We lost him in the system."

— NICK HAUPRICHT, TOLEDO-AREA VETERAN AND MEDAL OF HONOR RESEARCHER

ABOUT

- Born around 1844.
- Joined the Union Army at Toledo.
- Corporal in Co. D of the 124th Ohio Infantry.
- Awarded Medal of Honor for recapture of a U.S. guidon (flag) from a Confederate battery on Dec. 16, 1864, at Nashville, Tenn.
- Died Oct. 16, 1904. Thought to have moved to the Indian Territory, present day Oklahoma.

STARK CONNECTION

- Born in Stark County.

THE REV. DAVE LOMBARDI

"Brother Dave is one of those icon figures in the community. He is known for caring for the poor. We have worked with him on his food ministries. He gets calls from all over the world to his ministry. He has the heart to reach people with the love of God and message of Jesus Christ. He is still sharp, quick, vibrant. He is timeless."

— THE REV. DANA GAMMILL OF CATHEDRAL OF LIFE

ABOUT

- Born April 27, 1932, in Canton.
- Participated in founding what became Trinity Gospel Temple in 1964 in downtown Canton.
- Maintains an electronic media broadcast ministry known as Brother Dave and The Hour of Power Singers.
- Trinity Gospel Temple services are broadcast worldwide on The Church Channel, which is owned by Trinity Broadcasting Network.

STARK CONNECTION

- Trinity Gospel Temple holds services and maintains operations at 1612 Tuscarawas St. W, which is a former discount department store.
- Operates Camp Trinity in Perry Township.
- Brother Dave and The Hour of Power Singers can be heard on local contemporary Christian FM radio stations WNPQ and WOFN.

NADINE SECUNDE

"American singers will try anything. Even if they can't get it right, it won't be for lack of effort."

ABOUT

- Born Dec. 21, 1953, in Independence.
- Has performed in operas internationally.
- Debuted at the Bayreuth Festival in Germany in 1987, singing the role of Elsa in the Richard Wagner opera "Lohengrin."
- Debuted in America at the Lyric Opera of Chicago in another Wagner opera, "Tannhäuser."
- Graduated from the Oberlin Conservatory with bachelor of music in vocal performance and master of music in teaching and earned a master of music from Indiana University.

STARK CONNECTION

- Graduated from Hoover High School in 1970.
- Earned a Canton Civic Opera scholarship in 1974.

PERRY KING

"I was able to make a living as an actor for 35 years, which is almost an oxymoron."

ABOUT

- Actor who starred in the TV series "Riptide" (1983-86), and also appeared on "Almost Home," "Melrose Place," "Will & Grace" and "Spin City."
- Feature film credits include "The Day After Tomorrow," "The Lords of Flatbush," "The Possession of Joel Delaney" and "Mandingo."
- A 1984 Golden Globe best supporting actor nominee for the made-for-TV movie "The Hasty Heart."
- Received a degree in drama from Yale University and also studied drama at Juilliard.

STARK CONNECTION

- Born April 30, 1948, in Alliance.

ABRAHAM GREENAWALT

"He seldom referred to his army career and showed so little concern with that part of his life that his children know very little of its definite details."

— "A STANDARD HISTORY OF KANSAS AND KANSANS, VOLUME 4."
(ONE OF GREENAWALT'S SONS WAS A HOMESTEADER IN KANSAS).

ABOUT

- Born 1834, near Norristown, Pa.
- Bricklayer and farmer.
- Joined Union Army at Salem, Ohio.
- Private in Co. G of the 104th Ohio Infantry.
- Awarded Medal of Honor for capturing Confederate corps headquarters flag on Nov. 30, 1864, at Franklin, Tenn.
- One of five soldiers from the 104th to receive the Medal of Honor for their actions that day.
- Died 1922.

STARK CONNECTION

- Buried in Alliance City Cemetery.

79

EVA SPARROWGROVE

"The smallest good deed is better than the grandest intention."

— SPARROWGROVE, WHEN SHE RECEIVED THE JUNIOR LEAGUE OF STARK COUNTY'S WOMAN OF THE YEAR COMMUNITY AWARD IN 1952.

ABOUT

- Born in 1903. Died in 1985.
- Graduate of McKinley High School and Kent State University.
- Teacher for 48 years and known for writing hundreds of letters to former students, whom she called her "boys," during World War II. More than 100 of them wrote back.
- Made a silk banner stitched with the names of 310 of her former students who fought in World War II.

STARK CONNECTION

- Started teaching in Canton in 1925, first at Allen School

for 21 years, then at Timken High School for 6 years.
- Learned to speak Italian to better communicate with her students at Allen, many of whom came from immigrant families.
- Known to help her students with their car and mortgage payments as well as their college tuition.
- Recognized with many honors, including Woman of the Year, Volunteer of the Year and the Freedom Foundation Valley Forge Medal. She was added to the Stark County/Ohio Bicentennial Committee's Wall of Fame in 2003.

RUTH HARPOLD BASNER

"Numerous times she quenched our thirst for knowledge, and this is what made her so special."

— RICHARD McELROY OF JACKSON TOWNSHIP IN A LETTER TO THE EDITOR PUBLISHED IN THE REPOSITORY MARCH 10, 2006.

ABOUT

- Born Sept. 19, 1929. Died March 2, 2006.
- Member of North Canton High School's Class of 1947, and, according to her family, a graduate of The Principia in St. Louis, Mo., which is a school and college for Christian Scientists.
- Known as a local historian, and compiled the histories of many organizations.
- Served as past-president of the local history section of the Ohio Historical Society.

STARK CONNECTION

- Founded the North Canton Heritage Society and served as its executive director for 17 years.
- Penned various books, including "The North Canton Heritage, Vol. 1, 1805-1940" in 1972, and "Yesteryears: A Pictorial History of Stark County, Ohio" in 1998.
- Received multiple awards, including being among the first women to be selected for the Stark County Wall of Fame in 2002.

LEROY J. CONTIE JR.

"I admired his success and I wanted to follow in those steps."

— LEROY J. CONTIE JR., SAID ABOUT HIS FATHER, WHO WAS AN ATTORNEY.

ABOUT

- Born in 1920 in Canton; Died in 2001 in Cleveland.
- Was a U.S. Army sergeant from 1942 to 1946, serving during WWII.
- Nominated by President Richard Nixon in 1971 as judge for the U.S. District Court of the Northern District of Ohio.
- Nominated by President Ronald Reagan in 1982 as judge in the U.S. Court of Appeals for the 6th Circuit, the court only a step below the U.S. Supreme Court.

STARK CONNECTION

- Was law director in Canton in the 1950s and crusaded against prostitution, gambling and corruption.
- Served on the Stark County Board of Elections as a Republican representative in the 1960s.
- Was a Stark County Court of Common Pleas judge from 1969 to 1971.

JIM HOUSTON

"We all put our soul into playing for Massillon. You felt like you had to do your best for your teammates and team. For the city."

ABOUT

- Played 13 seasons as a defensive end and linebacker with the Cleveland Browns from 1960-72, making the Pro Bowl in 1964, 1965, 1969 and 1970. Helped the Browns win their last NFL title in 1964.
- Three-year starter at end at Ohio State, twice earning team MVP honors. Earned All-America honors in 1958 and 1959 and led the team in receiving in 1959.
- Elected to the College Football Hall of Fame in 2005 and was named to Ohio State's all-century team as a defensive end in 2000.

STARK CONNECTION

- Played end at Massillon from 1953-55 and is a member of the school's "Wall of Champions."

ROSA KLORER

"The hospital will be open to all. We will ask only two questions: 'Are you sick?' or 'Are you maimed?' "

— ROSA KLORER'S BROTHER, CHARLES F. LANG, IN 1908, IN ANNOUNCING THE GIFT THAT CREATED MERCY MEDICAL CENTER.

ABOUT
- Born Dec. 6, 1849, in Canton; died Aug. 1, 1938, in Canton.
- Honored with the Papal Cross by Pope Pius XI.
- Wife of Herman Klorer, one of the founders of Berger Manufacturing.

STARK CONNECTION
- Helped bring the Sisters of Charity of St. Augustine to Canton.
- Teacher at St. Peter's school.
- Purchased McKinley home in 1908 and deeded it for use as a hospital. That hospital today is known as Mercy Medical Center.

GUY MACK

"Put your guns down. There's a lot of people in this store here. Somebody's gonna get hurt; just put your guns down and get out of here."

— POLICE OFFICER GUY MACK DURING THE ROBBERY IN WHICH HE LOST HIS LIFE.

ABOUT
- Died July 22, 1972, at age 51.
- Hired in 1949 as a Canton police officer, advancing to detective; among a small number of black officers.
- Shot and killed when he intervened in an armed robbery while off duty and grocery shopping with his wife, Mabel, at the A&P store at 1800 Tuscarawas St E. Two of the three suspects were apprehended.
- Both suspects were convicted of murder and robbery and sentenced to life in prison.

- In 1974, both men agreed to identify the third suspect in exchange for reduced sentences. The third suspect was convicted and sentenced to life in prison.
- Mack is one of seven Canton officers killed in the line of duty. His photo hangs in the Police Department lobby.

STARK CONNECTION
- Lived on Schwalm Avenue NE in Canton.
- Member of St. Paul AME Church in Canton.

ABE M. LUNTZ

"It is a rare honor and privilege to be with you tonight upon the occasion of the National Brotherhood Banquet sponsored by the National Conference of Christians and Jews, and the presentation to A.M. Luntz of the National Human Relations Award, which he so richly deserves."

— PRESIDENT JOHN F. KENNEDY

ABOUT
- Born March 6, 1893. Died Feb. 24, 1981.
- After high school, he worked at his father's business, the Canton Iron and Metal Co.
- Abe and his brother, Darwin, founded a scrap metal firm in 1916, the Luntz Iron and Steel Co.
- Spurred by a scrap metal boom in WWI, the company expanded into Michigan, Pennsylvania and Kentucky.
- Named president of Luntz Iron and Steel in 1951.

STARK CONNECTION
- Moved to Canton with his family when he was around 6 years old.
- Graduated from Canton's Central High School in 1913.

ROBERT A. "BOB" HILL

"Bob is definitely a musical icon in the community. At age 81, he continues to still possess the same passion for music. ... He still has his own band and plays with many other bands in Stark County."

— BOB BLYER, CANTON

ABOUT
- Born Dec. 30, 1934.
- 1952 McKinley High School graduate who then received a music education degree in 1956 from Baldwin Wallace College.
- Trumpeter with U.S. Air Force Band in Washington, D.C.
- Retired as instrumental music instructor at Goodyear Junior High School in Akron.
- Arranged songs for two former Miss Ohio contestants for their appearances in Miss America pageant, including Laurie Lea Schaefer, who was Miss America in 1972.
- Conducted and arranged for an album, "Nice To Be Around," by nationally known singer Maureen McGovern.

STARK CONNECTION
- Resides in North Canton.
- Played in Canton Symphony Orchestra.

FRANK A. ZIMMER

"All his life has been spent in Canton and his personal history contains no pages marred or blotted by unworthy actions."

— FROM "OLD LANDMARKS OF CANTON AND STARK COUNTY" BY JOHN DANNER

ABOUT

- Born Sept. 7, 1872, in Canton; died 1953 in North Canton.
- Secretary/treasurer of Harvard Dental Manufacturing Co. for 40 years.
- Was organist at St. Joseph's Catholic Church for 20 years.
- Charter member of Canton Knights of Columbus.
- Leading voice in the Catholic Mutual Benefit Association.

STARK CONNECTION

- Attended parochial schools in Canton.
- For a time worked for B. Dannemiller & Sons wholesale grocers.
- Married Frances Kagle of Canton.

MARIE KEENER

"She was a doctor in a male dominated profession, but she was always a lady."

— NAN DEMUESY, FORMER PATIENT AND A GOOD FRIEND

ABOUT

- Born in Hartville to Benjamin and Anna Keener; died at age 106 in 2011 in the Canton area.
- Became interested in osteopathic medicine after a Canton doctor healed her mother's chronic bronchitis.
- Graduated from the Chicago College of Osteopathic Medicine in 1929.
- Knew Baroness Maria von Trapp, matriarch of von Trapp family whose story inspired "The Sound of Music," and Virgil Fox, an organist known for his interpretations of Bach.

STARK CONNECTION

- Practiced osteopathic medicine for 70 years in Stark County.
- Co-founded the former Doctors Hospital in Perry Township.
- Was a founding member of the International Soroptimist Club of Canton in 1941.
- Was active in numerous community organizations that included local camera clubs, the Canton Museum of Art, the Canton Audobon Society and the Humane Society of Stark County.

DONALD "DON" LUNDSTROM

ABOUT

- Born in 1933 in Canton.
- Attended Belle Stone School, McKinley High School and Ohio University, where he played baseball and graduated with degrees in mechanical engineering and commerce.
- Owner of Frankham Foundry until 1980.
- Sculptor of functional and artistic pieces using diverse materials including lost wax cast bronze, faceted slab glass, cement and aluminum.
- Since the 1970s, Lundstrom's work has been placed at sites throughout Ohio and elsewhere in the United States and Europe.
- Best of Show awards in wood and bronze sculptures, Boston Mills ArtFest and Hathaway Brown Fine Art Fair.

STARK CONNECTION

- Stark sculptures include "A Walk with the Boss" at North Canton square, "Garden Animals, Returning the Books" at North Canton Library, and "Seasons" at Aultman Hospital.
- Requested sculptor by North Canton Veteran's Memorial Committee.
- Past board member and officer for Canton Museum of Art.
- Enshrinee in Stark County Baseball Hall of Fame.

"Good night, Boss"

— WHAT DON LUNDSTROM SAID EACH EVENING AFTER WORKING ON HIS BOSS HOOVER BRONZE SCULPTURE.

BERNICE KEPLINGER McKENZIE FREASE

"Since an overwhelming majority voted for the lottery, I thought I should at least make sure it was well set up, honest and fair."

— BERNICE KEPLINGER McKENZIE FREASE IN 1973, WHEN SHE WAS APPOINTED TO SERVE ON THE OHIO LOTTERY COMMISSION.

ABOUT

- Born in Canton on Feb. 23, 1905.
- Died Oct. 10, 1990, at 85 in Canton.
- Graduated from McKinley High School in 1922, attended Mount Holyoke College, Canton Actual Business College and University of Akron Law School in 1932.
- First Canton woman to be admitted to Ohio State Bar in 1932.
- Appointed by Gov. John Gilligan in 1973 to the Ohio Lottery Commission, even though she had opposed legislation setting up the lottery.

STARK CONNECTION

- One of Stark County's first two women to be elected to the Ohio House of Representatives in 1940. The other was Ann Ryan. Frease served from 1941-42 and from 1958-66.
- Was an at-large Canton council member from 1956 to 1958.

EMERY A. McCUSKEY

"He had no desire for gain but only to serve. He was honest, incorruptible and the personification of integrity. In the practice of his profession, he acted on the basis of its highest standards."

— THE REV. ROLAND G. HOHN, OFFICIATING AT McCUSKEY'S FUNERAL

ABOUT

- Born near West Lafayette on Nov. 8, 1877; died June 21, 1952.
- Came to Canton in 1910 to practice law; became a senior member of Black, McCuskey, Souers & Arbaugh law firm.
- Active civic leader who served on the boards of many organizations; was president of Canton Public Library board; and was chairman of the committee that reorganized the YMCA.
- Served as chairman of the Canton Civil Service Commission.
- Chairman of the airport committee that laid the groundwork for Akron-Canton Airport.

STARK CONNECTION

- Member of the committee that organized what became Canton Regional Chamber of Commerce.
- Member of Canton's first charter commission in 1913.

ROBERT RAYMOND SCOTT

"This is my station and I will stay and give them air as long as the guns are going."

ABOUT

- Born July 13, 1915; died Dec. 7, 1941.
- Killed in the Japanese attack on Pearl Harbor.
- Machinists mate 1st class aboard the USS California.
- He refused to leave his station, manning an air compressor below deck after a torpedo hit, and went down with his ship.
- Buried in Arlington National Cemetery in Virginia.
- Awarded the Congressional Medal of Honor for "devotion to duty, extraordinary courage, and complete disregard for his own life, above and beyond the call of duty."

STARK CONNECTION

- Born in Massillon.
- Inducted in 2003 into the Stark County Wall of Fame.

WILLIAM R. THOM

"I see now more clearly than ever that if Germany and Japan were permitted to gain the goals they seek, they would together in the two oceans that touch us, some day spring upon us unawares, with the same devilish ingenuity that has marked the approach to our shores. That opportunity must not be given them."

— WILLIAM R. THOM, IN A STATEMENT FOLLOWING THE ATTACK ON PEARL HARBOR IN 1941

ABOUT
- Born July 7, 1885, in Canton; died Aug. 28, 1960.
- Attended Western Reserve University and Georgetown University Law School.
- Private secretary to Congressman John J. Whitacre, 1911 to 1913.
- Wrote for newspapers and was president of the National Press Club.
- Five-term Democratic member of the U.S. House of Representatives from Ohio's 16th District.
- Delegate to the 1956 Democratic National Convention.

STARK CONNECTION
- Popular Canton attorney.
- President of the Canton Park Commission.
- Buried in West Lawn Cemetery.

LEE WILKOF

"Everything nowadays is so much about celebrity, but there's a lot of us (actors) in the trenches. What defines being successful is different for every person."

ABOUT
- Born June 25, 1951, in Canton.
- New York stage actor who originated the leading role of Seymour in the original Off-Broadway production of "Little Shop of Horrors."
- A 2000 Tony Award nominee for "Kiss Me Kate." Other stage credits include "Assassins," "The Odd Couple" and "Sweet Charity" (all Broadway) and the national tour of "Wicked."
- Screen credits include the films "School of Rock" and "Howard Stern's Private Parts," and television series "Ally McBeal" and "Law & Order."
- Directed upcoming feature film "No Pay, Nudity" starring Nathan Lane and Gabriel Byrn.

STARK CONNECTION
- Graduated from Glenwood High School in 1969.
- Returned to Canton to play Seymour in "Little Shop of Horrors" for one night at a Players Guild benefit in 1993.

DAVID D. DOWD JR.

"He's brilliant, thoughtful and diligent in virtually every decision he made. He probably has as much or more respect than any jurist I can remember in my relatively long career."

— ATTORNEY JAMES L. BURDON, WHO BEGAN HIS LEGAL CAREER IN 1967

ABOUT

▪ Born in 1929 in Cleveland, grew up in Massillon.
▪ Received a bachelor of arts degree from College of Wooster in 1951 and a juris doctorate from the University of Michigan Law School in 1954.
▪ Appointed to the United States District Court for the Northern District of Ohio by President Ronald Reagan in August 1982. Previously served on court of appeals and was appointed to Ohio Supreme Court seat.

STARK CONNECTION

▪ Started the Dowd and Dowd law firm with his father,

David Dowd Sr., in Massillon in 1958. The partnership continued until 1975.
▪ Appointed assistant Stark County prosecuting attorney in 1961, and served until working as prosecuting attorney from 1967-1976.
▪ In 1981, joined Black, McCuskey, Souers & Arbaugh and was appointed to the U.S. District Court the following year.
▪ In 1988, he was appointed by the Judicial Conference of the United States to a four-year term on the Board for the Federal Judicial Center. He was appointed by Chief Justice William Rehnquist to serve on the Ad Hoc Asbestos Litigation Committee in 1990.

THE REV. JOHN ROBERT COLEMAN

"He was just a wonderful human being. His vision was expanding beyond the parish community into the entire northeast Canton community. It was a very positive outreach, caring about seniors and families that needed assistance."

— TOM THOMPSON, EXECUTIVE DIRECTOR OF JRC

ABOUT

▪ Born Aug. 18, 1933 in Canton.
▪ Helped start and lead St. Paul Social Action Committee, which eventually became JRC, a multifaceted, nonprofit providing social services in the Canton area.
▪ Ordained as a Catholic priest in 1960.
▪ Persevered during an uprising within the St. Paul's Catholic Church Parish Council to have the Diocese of Youngstown remove him as pastor over some disagreements regarding the priest's activities.

▪ Died Dec. 17, 1986 in Canton.

STARK CONNECTION

▪ Pastor of the former St. Paul's Catholic Church at 1530 Superior Ave. NE, Canton.
▪ St. Paul Social Action Committee was renamed JRC in Coleman's memory. JRC maintains JRC Adult Day Center at 3909 Blackburn Road NW, Plain Township; JRC Learning Center at 2213 14th St. NE; and JRC Senior Housing at 1732 Market Ave. N.

SISTER HENRIETTA GORRIS

"The Canton area is deep in the debt of this remarkable woman the nursing order in which she chose to spend her life ... to them and her assistants we are grateful beyond expression."

— THE REPOSITORY IN A 1962 ARTICLE ABOUT GORRIS' RETIREMENT FROM TIMKEN-MERCY HOSPITAL.

ABOUT

- Born Marie Gorris on July 19, 1902, in Cleveland. Died Oct. 17, 1983.
- In 1925, graduated from the Mercy Hospital School of Nursing in Canton as a registered nurse.
- Joined the Sisters of Charity of St. Augustine on Dec. 28, 1925, becoming Sister Henrietta.
- Known as "the Angel of Hough" for her work in the poverty-stricken Cleveland neighborhood, which was devastated by race riots in the mid-1960s.
- Converted an old apartment building in Hough into the Our Lady of Fatima Mission Center in 1965. Founded the CARIDAD and FAMICOS organizations.
- Received numerous awards and accolades for her work.

STARK CONNECTION

- Worked at Mercy Hospital and Timken Hospital from 1928 to 1962.
- Started as the night supervisor and later became supervisor of surgery, assistant administrator and administrator of Timken-Mercy.

MONSIGNOR EDWARD PATRICK GRAHAM

"You know, I think I should comb my hair or something. I feel like somebody is looking at me."

ABOUT

- Born July 1, 1862. Died March 15, 1944.
- Founded WHBC, a 10-watt radio station, on Feb. 13, 1925.
- WHBC made its broadcast debut on March 9, 1925, with a program hosted by Graham from St. John's sanctuary.
- License changed to St. John's parish in 1927; Graham continued to serve as station manager.
- Power increased from 10 to 100 watts in 1934.
- Graham sold the station to Brush-Moore Newspapers on Oct. 1, 1938.

STARK CONNECTION

- Pastor, St. John the Baptist Catholic Church, Canton, from 1922 to 1944.

HELEN WELSHIMER

"I spent my childhood speaking pieces on Children's Day, playing games with the neighborhood boys and girls, and being nice to the visiting clergy and missionaries."

ABOUT

- Born 1902; died in 1954.
- Journalist, magazine writer and nationally known poet.
- Published compilations of poems such as "Souvenirs," "Singing Drums," "Shining Rain" and "Candlelight."
- Her works of fiction include "Society Editor," "Love Without Music" and "Questions Girls Ask."
- In 1932, Welshimer won the first prize in poetry given by Ohio Newspaper Woman's Association.

STARK CONNECTION

- Born in Canton, the daughter of the Rev. P.H. Welshimer.
- Graduated from McKinley High School.
- Wrote for the Canton Daily News.

FRANK A. HOILES

"The Hoiles family was a very important and proud family in Alliance. They were business leaders, very enterprising, but also very generous."

—JACK PETERS, TO THE ALLIANCE REVIEW

ABOUT

- Born March 9, 1866, near Alliance.
- Died Dec. 29, 1936, at age 70 in car collision near Salem.
- Spent 42 years as publisher of the Alliance Review.
- Elected in 1903 as a Republican to the Ohio House of Representatives, serving 1904-08.
- Was president of the Alliance Brick Company, which owned plants in Alliance and Pennsylvania.

STARK CONNECTION

- Stark County native.
- Was on board of education for Alliance schools.

JOHN S. JOHNS

Industry "should not be content with simply making a profit without passing it along to wage earners and the community."

— FROM A 1964 SPEECH.

ABOUT

- Born in Beaver Falls, Pa., in 1915.
- An international vice president with the United Steelworkers from 1973 to 1977.
- Served as five consecutive four-year terms as director of Steelworkers District 27.
- Instrumental in Ohio working on the merger of the American Federation of Labor and the Congress of Industrial Organization to create the AFL-CIO, and served as vice president of the Ohio AFL-CIO.

STARK CONNECTION

- Family moved to Stark County in 1925.
- Became involved with the Steelworkers and trade unionism when he went to work at Republic Steel in 1933.
- One of the founders and the first president of the Amateur Sports Hall of Fame Association of Greater Canton.
- Served as trustee at Kent State University; vice president of the Canton Recreation Board; and member of the former Canton-North Canton Regional Transit Authority.

ELIZABETH "MIKE" CARMICHAEL

"Mrs. Carmichael's spare time must have a special elasticity because it is stretched to cover so many causes."

— REPOSITORY STORY

ABOUT

- Born: Harrisburg, Pa.
- Hair salon owner and operator; member of Ohio Beauticians Association; appointed to State Board of Cosmetology.
- Auditor with the Canton Income Tax Department
- Girl Scout leader, Red Cross and United Fund volunteer and Urban League Volunteer of the Year.
- Memberships in the Canton Negro Old-timers Association, Jane Hunter Civic Club, New Dawn Chapter of Order of Eastern Stars, Stark County branch of the NAACP, Stark County Mental Health Association, and Stark County Democratic Executive Committee.

STARK CONNECTION

- Moved to Canton in 1929.
- Attended St. Paul AME Church.

91

FRANK CUNNINGHAM JR.

"He served with great distinction and was highly respected and esteemed as both scholar and friend by his students and fellow faculty members."

— FROM HIS OBITUARY

ABOUT

- Born in Okolona, Miss., the oldest of 12 children, then raised in Canton.
- Received bachelor's degree from Mount Union College in Alliance; earned bachelor's in Sacred Theology, and master of arts and doctor of philosophy from Boston University.
- Did post-doctorate work at University of Hydraband in India on a Fulbright grant.
- Taught at Wilberforce University and Morris Brown College; rose to become president of Morris Brown.
- Was the first African-American elected to the presidency of the Georgia Philosophical Society.

STARK CONNECTION

- Graduated from McKinley High School in 1931.
- Was an ordained minister who was pastor at Christ Temple Church in Canton, which is now Greater Bethel Apostolic Church.

C. TED BRANIN

"I had the honor to be coached by and work for Mr. Branin at Branhaven Swim and Tennis Club. He had such a huge impact on me as a swimmer and a coach. I stress to my current Bulldog teams about the great tradition the Canton McKinley swim team had under Mr. Branin."

—McKINLEY HIGH SWIM COACH SAM SEIPLE

ABOUT

- Coached McKinley High's boys swimming team from 1928-1972, winning 13 state championships over that span — second-most in Ohio history. Also finished runner-up eight times.
- McKinley's natatorium is named after Branin. The facility has hosted every Ohio state boys swim meet since 1976 and every girls state meet since 1980. The pool opened in 1975 as a gift to Canton City Schools from the Timken Foundation.
- Coached the best swimmer in county history, Marty Mull, who won seven state titles in high school and was a two-time NCAA champion at Ohio State.

STARK CONNECTION

- A Dayton native, Branin accepted a teaching and coaching job at McKinley in 1928 after graduating college. He died in Canton at age 84 in 1988.

BEVERLY "BEV" BYRON KRAMMES

"My uncle was exactly the type of person you think of that would best represent the greatest generation."

— BRUCE JOHNSTON, NEPHEW, SAN ANTONIO, TEXAS

ABOUT

- Born April 17, 1914, in Newark, N.J.
- Died July 25, 1997, in Bradenton, Fla.
- Scout Leader for Boy Scouts of America
- Retired U.S. Marine Corps Reserve Colonel
- Awarded Distinguished Flying Cross for actions against Japanese forces in the Pacific Theater during World War II.

STARK CONNECTION

- Came to Stark County after war, working for Hoover Co. as a mechanical engineer
- Received patent for an electric flat iron and holder, which were signed over to Hoover.
- Moved to Florida in the late 1980s.

CARL O. WEIS

"Carl O. Weis has enjoyed his work because he knows you and I enjoy it, too, thinking of himself only as a public servant who had brought beauty for all to enjoy."

— THE REV. GEORGE E. PARKINSON AT THE DEDICATION OF A PLAQUE HONORING WEIS IN STADIUM PARK

ABOUT

- Born May 30, 1893, in Magnolia; died in 1979 in Canton.
- World War I veteran with the 145th Ambulance Company of the 37th Division.
- As parks superintendent and director for more than three decades, Weis grew the city park system from 120 acres to more than 800 acres.
- A bronze plaque honoring Weis was dedicated in Stadium Park in 1955, and Weis Park was named for him.
- Was active in Mason and veterans groups, and played clarinet in several area bands.

ALFRED E. RANSOM

"Ten Years From Now Is Today."

— SLOGAN DEVELOPED BY RANSOM TO ENCOURAGE CITY PLANNING FOR THE FUTURE OF THE CITY'S WATER NEEDS.

ABOUT

- Born Jan. 4, 1906, in Millersburg.
- Having an interest in music, Ransom sang over the radio in Cleveland and Cincinnati, then studied music in New York City at Carnegie Hall.
- Worked 43 years in the Canton Water Department, including years under Louis B. Ohliger, who is known as the "Father of Canton Water Works."
- Served as superintendent of the Water Department from 1932-34 and 1941-74.
- Doubled the size of Canton's water distribution to more than 500 miles of mains.
- Developed the Sugar Creek water field near Strasburg, built the Water Department headquarters and modernized the Al Ransom Well Field that bears his name.

STARK CONNECTION

- Family moved to Canton when he was 2.
- He attended Washington and Cherry Street schools and graduated in 1923 from McKinley High School.

DR. KARL BOYLE

"He taught a group of us calculus before it was ever in the school curriculum. It allowed me to skip two math classes at Ohio State."

— PAUL BISHOP, AT BOYLE'S INDUCTION TO LOUISVILLE HALL OF ACHIEVEMENT

ABOUT

- Math and science teacher, debate coach and assistant principal at Louisville High from 1940-1961.
- Started National Honor Society, National Forensic League at Louisville.
- In 1957, Louisville became first Ohio school to win a National Debate Championship, and Boyle's teams ranked second or third in national competition four times.
- In all, he qualified 31 students for national speech tournaments.
- Member of United States Hall of Fame for Speech and Debate Coaches.

STARK CONNECTION

- Born Dec. 17, 1917, in Malvern. Died April 3, 1999, in Louisville.
- Graduate of Marlboro High School.

BARBARA FAWCETT SCHREIBER

"I will remember Barbara as someone who was always well-prepared and intelligent."

— RANDOLPH SNOW, WHO SERVED ON THE BOARD WITH SCHREIBER,
AT THE TIME OF HER DEATH FOLLOWING A CAR CRASH.

ABOUT

- Born 1915; died 2002
- Graduated from McKinley High School in Canton and earned bachelor's degree from Connecticut College; attended Kent State University.
- Member of the Canton City Board of Education spanning four decades.
- Trustee of Ohio School Boards Association.
- Consultant to the directors of National Parent-Teachers Association.
- Junior League Woman of the Year in 1968.
- Member of the women's advisory council of Malone University and the women's committee of Walsh University.

STARK CONNECTION

- Spent her lifetime in Canton.
- Active in such local organizations as Girl Scouts, Junior League, College Club, Canton Recreation Board and Rotary Club.

WILLIAM BOWMAN

"The greatest thing is that they've been unsolicited. I never expected people to like a tax collector."

— WILLIAM BOWMAN, AT HIS RETIREMENT ABOUT THE COLLECTION OF ALMOST 100 ELEPHANTS PEOPLE
GAVE HIM FOR HIS OFFICE IN RECOGNITION OF HIS STATUS AS A REPUBLICAN COUNTY AUDITOR

ABOUT

- Born Feb. 25, 1930.
- Served as cryptographer in Army Signal Corps, 1951-53.
- Honored as distinguished alumnus of Alliance High School in 2010 and distinguished alumnus of Mount Union College in 1976.
- Alliance Citizen of the Year, 1977.
- After graduating from Mount Union in 1956, was general manager of Bowman Hardware of Alliance and worked as a broadcaster for WFAH radio.
- Served on Alliance City Council 1965-67.
- Deputy Stark County auditor, 1967-74; and Stark County auditor, 1974-91.

STARK CONNECTION

- Founding member of Mount Union Alliance Chorale and trustee of Canton Symphony Orchestra.
- Has given more than 3,200 musical programs in nursing homes, organizations and clubs, without asking payment.

JANETTE HENRY McAVOY McCLAVE

"She is not content to sit idly by but will go out of her way to help others ... She has always tried to put 110 percent into every phase of her life, whether it be teaching, community service, professional organizations or everyday living, and it truly shows in her accomplishments."

— McCLAVE'S DAUGHTER, MARYLEE THOMPSON

ABOUT

- Born March 13, 1912; died Oct. 5, 1996.
- Earned bachelor's and master's in education from Kent State University.
- Retired from Minerva Local Schools after years of teaching at Mary Irene Day Elementary School.
- Inducted in the Minerva High School Alumni Hall of Fame in 1991.
- One of the founders of the Minerva Historical Society and was a long-time community volunteer.
- Spent eight years on the Minerva Board of Education.

STARK CONNECTION

- 1924 graduate of Minerva High School.

CATHERINE L. NAU

"Your daughter has found ways of carrying on even under conditions that were never experienced before. One person with her spirit can keep up the morale of hundreds and thousands of others."

— A LETTER WRITTEN TO NAU'S MOTHER, ENGLINA NAU, BY LENA R. WATERS OF MILITARY AND NAVAL WELFARE SERVICE OF THE AMERICAN RED CROSS

ABOUT

- Graduated from the University of Pittsburgh; a social worker who later became assistant director of Philippine Red Cross field work.
- On Christmas Eve 1941, fled Manila for Bataan and then escaped with other nurses to the island of Corregidor.
- Became a Japanese prisoner of war Jan. 30, 1942.
- Liberated Feb. 23, 1945, by U.S. troops after 912 days in captivity.
- One of the "Angels of Bataan and Corregidor." The nurses kept U.S. soldiers in the camps alive and in good spirits, and cared for the sick, wounded and orphans.
- Awarded the Army Bronze Star medal in 1946.

STARK CONNECTION

- Born in Canton; died at 75 in March 1972 in Canton.

JOSEPH J. SOMMER

"All my life, I have been interested in Ohio's Natural Resources."

ABOUT

- Born July 9, 1927, in Canton.
- Served in U.S. Navy in 1945-46 in the Pacific Theater.
- Elected a Stark County commissioner from 1968-71.
- Proponent of Stark County Park District and charter member of Stark County Board of Park Commissioners.
- Served as assistant attorney general and deputy state auditor, as well as executive secretary of Ohio House of Representatives.
- Named director of Ohio Department of Natural Resources and served 1985-91.
- Inducted into Ohio's Natural Resources Hall of Fame in 1997.

STARK CONNECTION

- Lawyer in Stark County and also managed Kauffman Insurance Agency.
- Returned with his wife, Helen, to live in Stark County following his retirement in 1991.
- Sippo Lake Marina dedicated in his honor in 1985.

BLANCHE REED MOTTS

"When you work with Blanche, keeping up with her is the name of the game."

— DAVE FREITAG, THEN-PRESIDENT OF STARK COUNTY COUNCIL ON AGING, WHEN BLANCHE MOTTS RETIRED

ABOUT

- Born June 3, 1910; died April 27, 2000.
- Senior activities director at Downtown Canton YMCA for 22 years until her retirement at age 79.
- Initiated the effort to re-establish Senior Olympics in the Canton community.
- Instrumental in establishing Senior Boutique, Golden Wedding Dinner and Stark Senior Citizens Day.
- Junior League's Woman of the Year; Perry Rotary's Outstanding Senior Citizen; awarded Governor's Award for Community Service.
- Inducted into Area Agency on Aging Hall of Fame in 1992 and Ohio Senior Citizens Hall of Fame in 1998.

STARK CONNECTION

- Graduated from Malvern High School and Aultman School of Nursing.
- Worked as a registered nurse at Aultman Hospital and as a plant nurse at Hercules Engines.

GEORGE PAPADOPULOS

"George was greatly loved in Canton's Greek community. Like many of us, he came up from nothing."

— FRIEND ANTHONY MANOS, TO THE REPOSITORY ON JAN. 12, 1981

ABOUT

- Born on Aug. 3, 1927, in Canton.
- Died on Jan. 11, 1981, in Canton.
- Memorialized with stone marker in front of the Stark County Jail.
- Played cornet in local bands and often conducted the national anthem at Stark County Fair horse races.

STARK CONNECTION

- Became Stark County sheriff's deputy in 1950.
- Elected Stark County sheriff in 1967, and held office 13 years.
- President of National Sheriffs' Association and Buckeye State Sheriffs' Association.
- Lost contentious 1980 election to Republican Robert Berens.

EDWARD A. LANGENBACH

"From an investment of $300 in a small concern doing business in a room 14-by-16 feet in the loft of a building on Rex Ave. SE, he built up an industrial empire employing 10,000 persons at the time he retired 40 years later."

— THE REPOSITORY, SEPT. 9, 1930

ABOUT

- Born on Feb. 5, 1864, in Canton.
- Died on Sept. 8, 1934, at Congress Lake.
- Son of German immigrants.
- As general manager of United Steel Co., championed the development of vanadium-alloy steel for Ford's Model T in the early 1900s.
- Helped form Hercules Motors in 1915, and served as board chairman from 1930 to 1934.

STARK CONNECTION

- Canton-based industrialist and philanthropist.

ANDREW MEYER

"A favorite pastime for decades was a lazy afternoon at Meyers Lake, the crown jewel of Canton. The lake and the amusement park built on its shores were named for Andrew Meyer, who acquired it in 1817 as reparations for his help during the War of 1812."

— FROM "CANTON ENTERTAINMENT," BY KIMBERLY A. KENNEY

ABOUT
- Born in 1762 in Bonn, Prussia.
- Died June 27, 1848, in Canton.
- Immigrated to Baltimore in 1802.
- Fought with the United States in War of 1812; bought and outfitted two ships.

STARK CONNECTION
- Arrived in Canton in 1818.
- As compensation for lost warships, he was awarded land west of downtown.
- Expanded his property to 3,000 acres, which became Sweet Spring Farm, then Ohio's largest wheat farm.
- Meyers Lake named for him.
- Local legend has it that a strongbox, filled with gold, is buried on the grounds of the former Meyer estate, probably in the area that's now home to Lehman school.

SACRED TO THE MEMORY
OF
ANDREW MEYER
DIED JUNE 27, 1848
AGED 82 YRS

CORDELIA MEYER
DIED OCT 21 1847
AGED 74 YRS
REST IN PEACE

FRANK MERGUS

"The downtown Canton eatery was renowned for its creative approaches to the vegetables of the season ... Mergus' pea soup was a prime example. It wasn't the thick, pureed stuff of every other eatery. They simply boiled a few very fresh pea pods in a fine chicken broth and served it with the shelled peas in the bottom."

—THE REPOSITORY, IN A 2011 STORY

ABOUT
- Born Oct. 17, 1901, Arcadia, Greece. Died Aug. 6, 1980.
- Founding president of Mergus' Restaurant, a popular downtown Canton eatery he opened in 1943. The restaurant closed in 1983.
- Recipient, Tri-County Restaurant Association's Albert Julian Meritorious Service and Jesse H. Knight "Man of the Year" awards.
- Mergus' most famous employee was bartender Ferdinand Petiot, inventor of the "Bloody Mary."

STARK CONNECTION
- Moved to Canton from Detroit in 1922; married Canton native Ida K. Dannemiller in 1923.

99

RON BLACKLEDGE

"Timken gave me so much. My whole life belongs to Timken High School."

ABOUT

- Born April 15, 1938, in North Canton.
- Coached offensive line for the Pittsburgh Steelers from 1982-91. In 1988-89, his son, Todd, was a backup quarterback for the Steelers. Also served as an assistant coach for the Indianapolis Colts from 1992-97.
- Earned six varsity letters in football and baseball at Bowling Green, earning all-conference honors in both sports. Inducted into the school's athletic hall of fame in 1972.
- Went 8-25 as Kent State's head football coach from 1978-80.

STARK CONNECTION

- Earned first or second team All-Ohio honors in football, basketball and baseball at Timken High School, where he graduated in 1956.
- Spent 14 years as a head high school football coach at Canton South, Glenwood and Timken.

DON JAMES

"(I) feel very blessed to have been raised in Massillon and to be a part of that football tradition."

ABOUT

- Born Dec. 31, 1932, in Massillon.
- Died Oct. 20, 2013, in Kirkland, Wash.
- Played quarterback and defensive back for the University of Miami (Fla.) from 1951-53, setting five school passing records.
- Went 153-57-2 in 18 seasons as the head football coach at the University of Washington from 1975-92, leading the Huskies to a share of the 1991 national championship while winning four Rose Bowls and one Orange Bowl.
- Inducted into the College Football Hall of Fame in 1997.
- Went 25-19-1 as Kent State's head football coach from 1971-74, leading the Flashes to their only Mid-American Conference title in 1972. Also coached them to their first bowl game, the 1972 Tangerine Bowl.

STARK CONNECTION

- Quarterbacked Massillon from 1947-49, winning state titles as a junior and a senior.

THE REV. GEORGE E. PARKINSON

"During his life, Dr. Parkinson ... was instrumental in making grants to many local social service and cultural organizations."

— STARK COMMUNITY FOUNDATION

ABOUT

- Born: Nov. 27, 1912, in Fostoria. Died July 13, 1991.
- Pastor emeritus, Christ Presbyterian Church, Canton.
- Graduate of Otterbein College, Western Theological Seminary.
- Host of "The Cathedral Hour" weekly broadcast on WHBC Radio.
- Moderator of the Columbus, Mahoning and Wooster presbyteries; moderator, Synod of Ohio.
- Co-founder, Canton Council of Churches.
- 33rd Degree Mason; chaplain, Canton Police Department.

STARK CONNECTION

- Served Christ Presbyterian Church from 1943 to 1978.

JEFF BOALS

"I like to think of Jeff as a diversified coach. He's a terrific recruiter, understands in-game strategy and is relentless."

— AKRON MEN'S BASKETBALL COACH KEITH DAMBROT AFTER BOALS WAS HIRED AT STONY BROOK

ABOUT

- Born in Magnolia.
- Named head men's basketball coach at Stony Brook University in April 2016.
- Spent the previous seven seasons as an assistant coach at Ohio State, where he helped lead Buckeyes to three Big Ten titles, six NCAA tournament appearances and the 2012 Final Four.
- Also served as an assistant at Akron, Robert Morris, Marshall and Charleston.

STARK CONNECTION

- First team All-Ohio basketball player at Sandy Valley.
- Scored 1,064 points during his high school career.
- Two-year captain and four-year letterman at Ohio University, where he helped lead the Bobcats to an NCAA tournament appearance and the Preseason NIT championship.

PIERRE GARCON

"It does not seem like 10 years ago, but it's pretty cool to look back it and think I was out here. Every day I'm excited and happy about it. It was a blessing to come to Mount Union."

— GARCON, SPEAKING AT THE 2015 STAGG BOWL

ABOUT

- Born Aug. 8, 1986 in Carmel, N.Y.
- Has 485 receptions for 6,027 yards and 34 touchdowns over his eight-year NFL career with the Washington Redskins (2012-current) and Indianapolis Colts (2008-11), including a career year in 2013, when he led the NFL with 113 catches, breaking Art Monk's team record.
- Parents hail from Leogene, Haiti, a town near Port-au-Prince. Garcon was inspired to start his foundation, "Helping Hands," following the earthquake that hit the country in January 2010.
- A talented soccer player growing up, he began playing football as a high school junior in Greenacres, Fla., and didn't become a starter until his senior year.

STARK CONNECTION

- After playing one season at Norwich University in Vermont, transferred to Mount Union and set school records for career catches (202) and TD receptions (47) and finished second in career receiving yards (3,363) while leading the Purple Raiders to two Division III national titles.
- Became just the second Purple Raider to get drafted when the Colts selected him in the sixth round in 2008.

CHARLES R. HARRIS

"He was an inspiration to his family, friends, doctors and was a testimony to his faith."

— HARRIS' OBITUARY IN THE REPOSITORY IN 1990.

ABOUT

- Died Oct. 24, 1990, at 73 in Cambridge, Ohio, following a battle with cancer.
- Spent more than 20 years working with people with disabilities in Ohio.
- Retired in 1982 after serving as a supervisor of the Guernsey County Workshop for Retarded Persons.
- Charter member of the National Rehabilitation Association, the National Association of Retarded Persons and the Ohio Rehabilitation Association.

STARK CONNECTION

- Owned and operated with wife, Wilma Harris, Market Heights Pharmacy from 1947 to 1960.
- Taught special education at McKinley High School from 1960 to 1963.
- In 1963, he started the first workshop in Stark County for adults with developmental disabilities.
- Worked as a vocational rehabilitation supervisor for the Stark Mental Health Day Care Center.
- Selected as an enshrinee of the Stark County Wall of Fame in 2003.

RICHARD D. WATKINS

"He was the first to smile, shake your hand, say hello and really mean it."

— CANTON COUNCILMAN BILL SMUCKLER, D-AT LARGE, EULOGIZING THE LATE MAYOR WATKINS IN OCTOBER 2014.

ABOUT
- Born Sept. 16, 1930. Died Oct. 3, 2014.
- Graduated from Timken Vocational High School.
- Served in the U.S. Marine Corps.
- Known for his singing.

STARK CONNECTION
- Canton Ward 10 councilman for 10 years.

- Stark County commissioner from 1981-88, after his support of a county sales tax apparently led to his defeat.
- Elected Canton's mayor in 1991; served until 2003.
- Founder and president of Stark Enterprises for more than 50 years.
- As Canton's mayor, contributed to downtown revitalization, supporting demolition of buildings as part of the Streetscape project in the 1990s.

IRENE SMART

"Once you are elected, your job is to do what you were elected to do."

ABOUT
- Graduated from Harvard University with a degree in physical therapy.
- Entered William McKinley School of Law in 1953 as a married mother of two.
- Joined her husband's law practice and later became a local politician and judge.

STARK CONNECTION
- Now retired, lives in Jackson Township.

- Served as a Democrat for 13 years on Canton City Council and five years in the Ohio House of Representatives.
- Elected in 1977 as Canton municipal judge, becoming the first woman municipal court judge in Stark County.
- Served as judge for Stark County Common Pleas Court and the 5th District Court of Appeals, where she stayed from 1988 to 1995. She was the first female on the appeals court.

J. BABE STEARN

"There are several dimensions to his life. For a Jewish person to become sheriff was very rare. Obviously, he was loved by the community. He had a tremendous love for children. There was no place in the county he could go where people didn't recognize him."

— RABBI EMERITUS JOHN SPITZER OF TEMPLE ISRAEL

ABOUT

- Born: March 20, 1914, in Kovena, Russia. Died: Jan. 11, 2007.
- Former lieutenant, Canton Police Department.
- First elected Stark County sheriff in 1984 as a Democrat.
- Coached boxing at the former National Guard Armory, which later became the Police Boys Club in the southwest section of Canton.
- Helped launch the local Mitey Mite youth baseball program.

STARK CONNECTION

- Served two terms as Stark County sheriff.
- J. Babe Stearn Community Center at 2628 13th St. SW was named in his honor.

BOB HUGGINS

"I got in a truck with this guy one time and looked and he didn't have a rear-view mirror. I said, 'You don't have a rear-view mirror.' He said, 'I don't back up. We're going forward, son.' And that's kind of how I've lived my life."

ABOUT

- Born Sept. 21, 1953, in Morgantown, W.Va.
- Has spent 31 seasons as an NCAA Division I men's basketball coach, including the last nine at West Virginia.
- Led teams to the NCAA tournament 22 times, including Final Fours while at Cincinnati in 1992 and at West Virginia at 2010.
- Coached Akron to its first NCAA tournament appearance as a Division I program in 1986.

STARK CONNECTION

- Compiled at 71-26 record as the head coach at Walsh College from 1980-83.
- Led the Cavaliers to two NAIA postseason berths, including their first national tournament appearance in 1983.
- Guided the 1982-83 Walsh team to a 30-0 regular season and a No. 2 national ranking.

OSCAR GRIMES

"Oscar Grimes, played in the bigs for nine seasons, from 1938-46. The infielder played for Cleveland, the Yankees and the Philadelphia A's, making the 1945 All Star team for New York, but not playing. That season, Grimes wore No. 7, now Mickey Mantle's retired number."

— GAMMONSDAILY.COM

ABOUT
- Born April 13, 1915. Died May 19, 1993.
- Made major league debut Sept. 28, 1938, with Cleveland Indians.
- Played final game Sept. 25, 1946.
- In nine MLB seasons, batted .256 with 18 homers and 200 RBI.
- Made putout at first base to end Joe DiMaggio's 56-game hitting streak in 1941.
- Played with DiMaggio, Yogi Berra, Tommy Heinrich on 1946 New York Yankees team.
- Father Ray Grimes and uncle Roy Grimes played in major leagues.

STARK CONNECTION
- 1938 graduate of Minerva High School.

RUSS KIKO

"Russell believed in keeping his business clean, and as a result, he drew a large following of admirers. This honest and straightforward way of conducting business led to recognition from his peers."

— OHIO CONGRESSMAN JAMES A. TRAFICANT JR.

ABOUT
- Founded Russ Kiko Associates in 1945, running auctions on Fridays out of his Canton Township barn.
- Always held an absolute auction, where the seller agrees to accept the sale price regardless of the amount.
- First Ohioan inducted into National Auctioneers Association Hall of Fame; among first group inducted into Ohio Auctioneers Association Hall of Fame.
- Was named chair of a temporary national farmers' organization, called the National Quota Protesting Association, which was formed to oppose wheat marketing quotas and other crop restrictions.

STARK CONNECTION
- Lived in the Canton and Minerva areas.
- Had 13 children with wife, Coletta, and the children eventually took over the Stark County business.

THOMAS REES MORGAN SR.

"No words can too highly praise the personal character of Thomas R. Morgan Sr. He was a noble man, a true friend, an upright, progressive, patriotic and enterprising citizen. His loss will be keenly felt."

— STATE SEN. SILAS WILLIAMS, UPON HEARING OF MORGAN'S DEATH, AS QUOTED IN THE EVENING REPOSITORY SEPT. 7,1897.

ABOUT

- Born March 31, 1834, in Glamorgan, Wales.
- Died Sept. 6, 1897, in Alliance.
- Immigrated to America in 1865, first settling in Pittston, Pa.
- By 1868, he was superintendent of several shops, including the Allegheny Valley Railroad.
- Founded company in Pittsburgh in 1868, making steam hammers and other machinery.
- Moved his business, then called Marchand & Morgan, to Alliance in 1871.

STARK CONNECTION

- In 1884, company was renamed Morgan Engineering.
- In its early years, his company was a pioneer in developing overhead cranes.
- A 25-ton double trolley overhead crane was exhibited at the Chicago World's Fair in 1893.
- In 1894, Morgan Engineering produced a disappearing gun carriage, the largest ever built in the U.S.
- Upon Morgan's death, most of the company was willed to his son, William. His three brothers sold their shares.

T.K. HARRIS

"Everything had to be perfection."

— JACK WYNN, HARRIS' SON-IN-LAW, FOR A 2010 STORY IN ABOUT MAGAZINE. WYNN WENT ON TO DESCRIBE HOW A CHAUFFEUR REGULARLY DROVE HARRIS AROUND THE VILLAGE IN SEARCH OF "ANY STONE OUT OF PLACE."

ABOUT

- Born April 28, 1882, in Lawrence, Kan.
- Died Nov. 17, 1958 in Hills and Dales.
- Moved to Canton when he was 5, after the death of his father.

STARK CONNECTION

- One of the founders of Brookside Country Club.
- Founder of Canton Real Estate Board.
- Developer responsible for Hills and Dales Village and Tam O' Shanter golf course.
- Built the Harris Arcade in downtown Canton (now the vacant Kresge lot).
- His majestic Hills and Dales Tudor house still is known as the T.K. Harris home.
- Local commercial real estate firm still bears his name.
- Served as a mayor of Hills and Dales.

GEORGE MONNOT

"However a man who knows what it is to be up and down can fully appreciate the spirit of one who has gone through the same ordeal," he wrote to a Good Samaritan who'd given him $5 for Christmas.

— SMITHSONIAN.COM QUOTING MONNOT, WHO LOST EVERYTHING DURING THE GREAT DEPRESSION, WROTE A LETTER OF THANKS TO A BENEVOLENT MAN WHO'D GIVEN HIM $5, MONEY HE'D SPEND ON SHOES FOR HIS DAUGHTERS AND "OTHER LITTLE NECESSITIES."

ABOUT
- Born Sept. 29, 1873, in Canton.
- Died Feb. 27, 1949, in Canton. He is buried in St. John's Cemetery.
- Invented the Hydrocar, a vehicle built in 1917 to move through the water using a four-cylinder Hercules engine. The Hydrocar is listed in The Standard Catalog of American Cars 1805-1942.

STARK CONNECTION
- Co-owner of Monnot & Sacher, whose dealership often featured a band with 11 players sporting tuxedos.
- Opened a bicycle shop, but went on to open the city's first Ford dealership.

RHODA WISE

"I believe Rhoda was a humble, simple woman whom our Lord gave graces to."

— KAREN SIGLER, DIRECTOR OF THE RHODA WISE HOUSE & GROTTO

Her Name Means Rose

The Rhoda Wise Story

Karen Sigler S.F.O.

ABOUT
- Born Rhoda Greer on Feb. 22, 1888, in Cadiz, the sixth of eight children.
- Introduced to Catholicism at 16 when a nun gave her a St. Benedict medal after an appendectomy.
- A mystic and stigmatic who experienced miraculous healings and visitations from Jesus and "The Little Flower," St. Therese of Lisieux, in the 1930s and 1940s. When word got out, thousands of people descended upon the house every week to see her.
- She reported that Jesus first visited her twice in the hospital, healing what doctors said was incurable stomach cancer and then a broken foot.

STARK CONNECTION
- Married and moved to Canton in November 1915.
- Lived at 2337 25th St. NE.
- Died July 7, 1948. More than 14,000 attended her funeral Mass. She is buried at St. Peter's Cemetery.

CARLIN ISLES

"I've never seen anyone that quick on a rugby field ever, XV's or Sevens. I don't think anyone else has either."

— LONGTIME BRITISH RUGBY PROFESSIONAL PLAYER, JOURNALIST AND COMMENTATOR NIGEL STARMER-SMITH

ABOUT
- Born in Massillon.
- Made it to the Olympic trials as a sprinter in 2012.
- Took up rugby shortly after and quickly earned the title "Rugby's Fastest Man."
- Member of the US Sevens National Team that qualified for the 2016 Olympics.

STARK CONNECTION
- Standout football player and track and field athlete at Jackson High School.
- Still holds the school records in the long jump, 100, 200, 400 and 800 relay at Jackson.
- Went on to compete in track and field at Ashland University, where he still holds freshman records in the 100, 200 and 400.

WAYNE FONTES

"We gave you guys some hope. When we came here, we never had that."

— FONTES IN 1996, AFTER HE WAS FIRED AS HEAD COACH OF THE LIONS.

ABOUT
- Born Feb. 2, 1940, in New Bedford, Mass.
- Recorded four interceptions in nine games as a defensive back for the American Football League's New York Titans in 1962, his only pro season.
- Spent 13 seasons as an assistant coach in the NFL, including seven as defensive coordinator of the Tampa Bay Buccaneers and Detroit Lions.
- Head coach of the Lions from 1989-96. Named NFL Coach of the Year in 1991 after he led Detroit to a 12-4 record and the NFC Championship Game.

STARK CONNECTION
- Played football, basketball and baseball at McKinley High School.
- Helped lead McKinley to a 20-0 record and back-to-back state football championships in 1955 and 1956.
- Ranks sixth on the Bulldogs' single-season scoring list with 146 points in 1956.
- Elected to the Stark County High School Football Hall of Fame in 2003.

GEORGE HERMAN JOHNSON

"Our purpose isn't to turn out great actors or actresses, but to develop poise, interest and reliability in members of our group."

ABOUT
- Wrote a volume of 200 poems titled "Why."
- Started the Negro Little Theater in Massillon in 1936.
- Had 30 "finished" actors by 1940 who had performed major productions and other smaller plays
- Was a member of the Negro Civic Council, Fort Knight Club, the Nation Youth Movement and the Square Deal Club.
- Directed the Urban League.

STARK CONNECTION
- Attended elementary school in Canton.
- Was featured in a 2006 Massillon Public Library exhibit about the most notable black people in the city's history.

VINCENT W. SHUPE

"He could hit good, but he couldn't run worth a darn. I could have beaten him running backwards."

— TIM TRINER, A FORMER BASEBALL TEAMMATE OF VINCENT SHUPE

ABOUT
- Born Sept. 5, 1921 in East Canton.
- Died April 5, 1962, of a heart attack while bowling in Canton.
- Played first base for the Boston Braves in 1945, debuting July 7 and playing 78 major league games, batting .269 with 15 RBI, three stolen bases and 16 strikeouts.
- Batted around .350 in 1941 for the Johnstown Johnnies (the Brooklyn Dodgers' Class D affiliate) in the Pennsylvania State Association.
- Played in 1950 for the Oklahoma City Indians (Class AA affiliate of the Cleveland Indians) in the Texas League.
- Dated actress Jean Peters, a Stark County native who married billionaire Howard Hughes.

STARK CONNECTION
- Graduated from East Canton High School in 1939.
- Buried in Mapleton Cemetery in Osnaburg Township.

HARRY J. "DOC" GUIST

"I would like nothing better than to get rid of the need for more dentists — then I'm going to have to find a new job."

— GUIST EXPLAINING WHY HE SUPPORTED PUTTING FLUORIDE IN THE CITY'S WATER, AS RECALLED BY FORMER MAYOR RICHARD WATKINS.

ABOUT

- Born March 25, 1922, in Apollo, Pa.
- Died Nov. 19, 2007, in Canton.
- Trained as Army Air Corps pilot in World War II.
- Studied at University of Alabama and Kent State University; earned degree as doctor of dental surgery from Western Reserve University in 1949.

STARK CONNECTION

- Canton Ward 6 councilman for 14 years. Was proponent of placing fluoride in city's water, a municipal income tax and construction of a new city hall.
- McKinley High School graduate, captain for state champion swimming team.
- Practiced as a dentist in Canton for 42 years.
- President of the Canton Jaycees.
- Developed Mother Gooseland nursery rhyme theme park.

LUKE WITTE

"He teaches kids about respect. He teaches them about courage and strength. He also covers nutrition. His camp is more about basketball. It's about life as it is as much about sports."

— MARLBORO CHAPEL SPORTS PASTOR TODD HOSTETLER ON WITTE'S ANNUAL BASKETBALL CAMP HE CONDUCTS AT THE CHAPEL.

ABOUT

- Born in Philadelphia.
- Went on to play college basketball at Ohio State.
- Drafted by and played four years for the Cleveland Cavaliers.
- Currently is the Carolinas Division director of Marketplace Chaplains.

STARK CONNECTION

- The 7-foot Marlington High grad was one of the most prolific scorers in county history, with more than 1,500 points.
- Led Ohio State in rebounds as a sophomore with 331.
- Witte was attacked and subsequently stomped by several Minnesota players during an ugly on-court brawl his junior year.

LOUIS HOICOWITZ

"Houses designed by Hoicowitz used unusual building materials and showed a love of detail in design and in construction."

— HISTORIC RIDGEWOOD DOCUMENT THAT DETAILS THE HISTORY OF THE ALLOTMENT
WHERE THE MORE AFFLUENT CANTON RESIDENTS LIVED DURING THE 1920S AND '30S

ABOUT

- Born July 15, 1890, in Vitebsk, Russia.
- Died May 1, 1976, in Canton.
- Immigrated to Stark County from Russia to go into business with a friend, but opened his own construction company when that partnership fell through.

STARK CONNECTIONS

- Owned and operated Louis Hoicowitz

Construction Co., founded in 1922.
- Built more than a dozen homes in Canton's historic Ridgewood neighborhood, ranging from Georgian Revival style to Tudor. His French Norman Revival work was his best.
- Designed chimneys with free-standing separate shafts with corbelled caps at the top. Turrets were topped by conical roofs.
- Designed and built Temple Israel.

LARRY KEHRES

"Coach Kehres has been an incredible success, not only in winning football games and national championships at an unprecedented level, but also in positively shaping the lives of countless student-athletes."

— UNIVERSITY OF MOUNT UNION PRESIDENT RICHARD GEISE

ABOUT

- Born Sept. 7, 1949, in Diamond.
- Earned bachelor's in business administration from Mount Union in 1971 and master's in health and physical administration from Bowling Green State University.

STARK CONNECTION

- Quarterback for Mount Union from 1967-70.

- College coach to win 300 games in the shortest amount of time, compiling overall mark of 332-24-3 (.929).
- Became Mount Union head football coach in 1986, coached 27 seasons (1986-2013).
- His Mount Union teams won 11 NCAA Division III national championships.
- Mount Union's athletic director in his 42nd year at the university.

TOMMY JAMES

"I played against a lot of great players from Stark County and a lot of Hall of Famers in the NFL. I was pretty fortunate."

ABOUT

- Born Sept. 16, 1923, in Massillon. Died Feb. 7, 2007, in Massillon.
- Played halfback at Ohio State from 1941-42, helping the Buckeyes win their first national title in 1942. After serving three years in the Army during World War II, he returned to Ohio State for the 1946 season.
- Played 10 seasons of professional football with the Detroit Lions (1947), Cleveland Browns (1948-55) and Baltimore Colts (1956), winning two AAFC titles and three NFL titles as a defensive back. Made the Pro Bowl in 1953.

STARK CONNECTION

- Played quarterback and halfback at Massillon from 1938-40, going 30-0 with three straight state titles. Over his three years with the Tigers, they outscored opponents 1,239-91, including 477-6 his senior year.

BOB BOLDON

"He has done a remarkable job in all facets of his job. He is building something special. The future of our women's basketball program is very bright under Bob's leadership."

— OHIO UNIVERSITY DIRECTOR OF ATHLETICS JIM SCHAUS, AFTER BOLDON SIGNED A FIVE-YEAR CONTRACT EXTENSION IN 2015

ABOUT

- Born April 30, 1975.
- Head women's basketball coach at Ohio University since 2013, leading Bobcats from 6-23 season in 2012-13 to a program-record 27 wins, MAC regular-season and tournament championships and NCAA tournament berth in 2014-15; MAC Coach of the Year, 2014-15 season.
- Head women's basketball coach at Youngstown State from 2010-13; Horizon League Coach of the Year, 2012-13, when team won 23 games and a WNIT berth.
- Also served as head coach at NAIA Lambuth and NCAA Division II Arkansas-Monticello.

STARK CONNECTION

- Played high school basketball at Louisville. Named Northeastern Buckeye Conference Player of the Year in 1992-93.
- Four-year-starting point guard at Walsh University, where he scored 1,694 points and handed out a school-record 775 assists.
- Two-time NAIA All-American and Mid-Ohio Conference Player of the Year. Helped lead the Cavaliers to the NAIA Final Four in 1996.
- Assistant women's basketball coach at Walsh in 1998, when the Cavs won an NAIA national championship.

ALFRED NICKLES

"Nickles often fondly recalled his days as an apprentice, when he walked through the streets of Paris, peddling a bag full of baked goods slung across his shoulder."

— FROM A DEC. 27, 1930, STORY IN THE CANTON REPOSITORY

ABOUT

- Born in 1884, in Iens, Switzerland.
- Died June 28, 1949, in Cleveland.
- Began as an apprentice baker at age 13, in Switzerland and in Paris.
- Immigrated to the U.S. in 1903 at age 19.
- Opened and failed in bakeries in Uhrichsville, Akron and Cleveland.

STARK CONNECTION

- Founded Navarre Bakery and Ice Cream (which became Alfred Nickles Bakery) in Navarre in 1909.
- Wife, Emma, and her sister, Ida Baumgardner, were first employees.
- Company incorporated in 1934.
- Nickles today consists of three modern bakeries and 37 distribution branches. The company is a leading wholesale baker and distributor of bread, rolls, and sweet goods.

SHERLOCK HOLMES EVANS

"Every time I check into a hotel, I sign my name Sherlock Holmes Evans. I like to see the clerk look over his shoulder and wonder why I didn't sign 'Smith.'"

ABOUT

- Born 1906 in Massillon; died 1987.
- Attorney, author, humorist, actor, circus performer.
- Graduate of Academy of Dramatic Arts and Columbia University, William McKinley School of Law, Cleveland Law School.
- Autobiography, "Father Owned a Circus," and performer, J.J. Evans Society Circus.
- Honorary member, International Mark Twain Society.
- Assistant field director for the Red Cross during World War II.
- Made more than 100 speeches a year.

STARK CONNECTION

- Massillon Municipal Court clerk, city solicitor, chief deputy for Judge Reuben Z. Wise.
- Active in local civil-rights causes.

KERI SARVER

"It's such a part of who I am. It's a passion and love I have for the game of soccer, all aspects of it."

ABOUT

- Born March 30, 1976.
- Played professional soccer for the Cleveland Eclipse, Washington Freedom, New York Power and Carolina Courage.
- Two-time All-ACC player at Maryland and selected to ACC 50th anniversary team.
- Terps' career leader in points (155), goals (61) and assists (33).
- Member of Ohio Soccer Hall of Fame.

- Has coached on various levels; now director of coaching for Internationals Soccer Club.

STARK CONNECTION

- Graduated from Jackson High School in 1995.
- Scored 50 goals as a senior at Jackson and led team to state semifinals.
- Three-time All-Ohioan and a Parade All-American for Polar Bears.

FRANCIS ONESTO

"The speakers all praised the hotel ... but most of all, they praised Francis Onesto, who came to their city a poor boy without friends or acquaintances and who for 10 or more long years had dreamed of the hotel he would build."

— HOTEL BULLETIN, A NATIONAL PUBLICATION FOR THE LODGING INDUSTRY

ABOUT

- Born Aug. 1, 1892, in New Castle, Pa. Died July 29, 1958, in the McKinley Room of the Hotel Onesto during a meeting of the Downtown Development Company.
- Traveled from Wooster to Canton at age 14 in the summer of 1907.
- In August 1930, he opened the 14-story Hotel Onesto at Second Street and Cleveland Avenue NW in downtown Canton at a cost of $1.2 million; the project included investors.

- President John F. Kennedy and Eleanor Roosevelt visited the Onesto. Celebrities who stayed there include Jimmy Stewart, Woody Hayes, Marilyn Monroe and Howard Hughes.

STARK CONNECTION

- Worked at the Delmont Restaurant in Canton as a teenager before purchasing the business.
- The former hotel building has reopened as the Historic Onesto Lofts, upscale apartments.

JAMES PURCELL RODMAN

ABOUT

- Born in Alliance Nov. 11, 1926; died Jan. 2, 2015.
- Graduated from Western Reserve Academy, then Mount Union with a triple major in physics, mathematics and chemistry.
- Earned his master's in experimental nuclear physics from Washington University in St. Louis and doctorate in astrophysics at Yale University.
- Designed, wired and installed the lighting system for Rodman Theater; conceived and constructed radio station WRMU; founded, engineered and ran Mount Union's first computer center.
- Rebuilt and refurbished the Clarke Observatory, then designed and constructed the Rodman Observatory in Alliance.
- Installed Mount Union's campus walkway lighting system, and designed and underwrote the Eckler Garden on the campus.

STARK CONNECTION

- Was a physics professor, head of the physics department, and staff astronomer at Mount Union.
- Served as president of Alliance Board of Education and was a member of the boards of Alliance Community Hospital, Alliance YMCA and Alliance Community Concert Association.

CASSANDRA CROWLEY

"It's exciting. We're now getting the kids of dancers I taught when they were kids. It's really fun to see them grow up and see how much they're like their parents and how much not."

ABOUT

- Born 1955 in Tacoma, Wash.
- Her mother enrolled her in ballet lessons at age 13 because she was a tomboy.
- Studied ballet in London, England, and Cannes, France, then danced ballet professionally for three years in Ljubljana, Slovenia.
- Was hired in 1980 as director of the School of Canton Ballet, and in 1981 became the company's artistic director.
- A founder and director emeritus of Regional Dance America, a national organization for pre-professional dance companies.
- Will begin staging Canton Ballet performances at the Cultural Center's Black Box Theatre in 2017.

STARK CONNECTION

- Launched a holiday production of "The Nutcracker" at Canton's Palace Theatre that has played annually, averaging 5,500 attendance yearly.
- Crowley alumni who have gone onto professional careers include Zachary Catazaro (New York City Ballet), Kelly Yankel (Sarasota Ballet), Anne Shaheen (Ohio Ballet) and Tommie Jenkins ("Cats," Jersey Boys").

JERRY GOODPASTURE

"Every year is different. I like the competition. I like coaching the young kids. I guess you could say they keep me young."

ABOUT
- Born Feb. 11, 1939.
- Earned bachelor of science in education from Kent State University, taught American history at Hoover High School from 1971-1998.
- Played catcher for Golden Flashes from 1957-1961.

STARK CONNECTION
- Hoover softball assistant/head coach since 1985.
- Became Hoover High head softball coach in 2005.
- Coached Vikings to Division I state championships in 2006, 2008, 2011-14.
- Overall record is 326-49 in just 12 seasons
- Coached two of Ohio's greatest prep pitchers in Katie Chain and Jessica Simpson.

BRUCE BEATTY

"New special teams coach Bruce Beatty is linked with two of pro football's most hallowed shrines: Canton and Miami, Ohio."

— BUFFALOBILLSANNUALINFORMATION.COM

ABOUT
- Born June 15, 1928.
- First team All-Ohio, All-County, All-City end/tackle for Lincoln High School in 1945.
- Spent 18 seasons as an offensive line coach for Ara Parseghian at Miami of Ohio and Northwestern.
- NFL offensive line coach for New England (1969-72), Houston Oilers (1973-74), Detroit Lions (1975-76); and special teams coach for Buffalo Bills (1977).
- Coached in the AFL, NFL, USFL and the German Football League.

STARK CONNECTION
- Star on Lincoln's 1945 7-0-3 football team that tied McKinley, 7-7; Massillon, 0-0; and played No. 1 Toledo Waite to a 0-0 draw in a Dec. 1 state championship game at Fawcett Stadium.

JOHN MAHON

"Sometimes it is the glamorous rock 'n' roll lifestyle, but it's also a lot of work."

ABOUT

- Born Jan. 23, 1955, in Canton.
- 1973 graduate of St. Thomas Aquinas High School.
- Has been a percussionist and backing vocalist in Elton John's touring band since 1997.
- Biggest concerts include five-night stand at Madison Square Garden, Carnivale in Rio (100,000 people), Coliseum in Rome (over 200,000 people), Hyde Park in London (500,000 people).

- Mahon also has toured with Al Stewart, Rita Coolidge and Helen Reddy.

STARK CONNECTION

- At Aquinas, played drums in the marching, concert and jazz bands and sang in the school choir.
- Was honored in 2010 as a distinguished alumnus in a ceremony at Aquinas.
- Married since 1980 to Canton native Pam Tortola, with whom he lives in Southern California.

GARY L. WILSON

"Leadership and management are a business's most important asset. They are not on the balance sheet, but they can quickly produce results. Be aggressive about who you work for and hire people better than you are."

— GARY L. WILSON DURING A SPEECH IN 2005 AT THE UNIVERSITY OF SOUTHERN CALIFORNIA

ABOUT

- Spearheaded the 1989 buyout of Northwest Airlines and became co-chairman of the airline company in 1991. He served as chairman from 1997 to 2007, during which he oversaw the acquisition of Continental Airlines.
- Joined Walt Disney Co. in 1985 and served as executive vice president and chief financial officer until 1990. He continued as a director until 2006.
- Executive vice president for finance and development at Marriott Corp. from 1974 to 1985, where he has been credited with developing the Courtyard Hotel concept.

STARK CONNECTION

- Graduated from Alliance High School in 1958.
- Established the Elvin J. Wilson- Duke University Scholarship in 1998 in memory of his father, a businessman and who served as an Alliance councilman-at-large. The scholarship is awarded annually to an Alliance High School student who is enrolling at Duke University. Duke pays half of the scholarship with Wilson contributing the other half.

117

KOSTA KOUFOS

"He's just a pro. … I mean, he's one of my favorite stories of all the guys I've coached."

— VETERAN NBA COACH GEORGE KARL, WHO COACHED KOUFOS IN DENVER AND SACRAMENTO

ABOUT

- Eight-year NBA veteran has played for the Jazz, Nuggets, Grizzlies and Kings.
- First-round draft pick (23rd overall) by the Jazz in 2008.
- Played one year at Ohio State and was named MVP of the NIT.
- Dual American-Greek citizen who plays for Greece's national team.

STARK CONNECTION

- Born Jan. 24, 1989, in Canton to Kathy and the late Alex Koufos.
- Graduated in 2007 from GlenOak High School, where he scored 1,297 career points.
- McDonald's All-American as a senior at GlenOak, led Golden Eagles to a state semifinal.

DR. GRACE HOFSTETER

"I always enjoyed working with the hands and making diagnoses."

— DR. GRACE HOFSTETER, IN A 1988 INTERVIEW

ABOUT

- Born Feb. 3, 1926; died March 21, 2016.
- Innovator and leader in the field of heart care.
- Graduated from Massillon Washington High School, College of Wooster and University of Maryland School of Medicine, then trained at Mercy Hospital and Cleveland Clinic.
- Opened the cardiac catheterization lab in Timken Mercy Hospital and helped start the coronary care unit at the hospital.
- Is credited with performing the first heart catheterization in a community hospital in 1957.
- Reported to be the first doctor in Stark County to insert a temporary pacemaker.
- Is credited with being the first person in the county to successfully use a defibrillator to revive a coronary seizure victim.

STARK CONNECTION

- Lived in Canton most of her life.
- Was medical director at House of Loreto and co-founded the Ohio Medical Directors Association.

MARY MERWIN

"I think what stood out for her as a director was that she demanded excellence."

— MARGY VOGT, PUBLIC RELATIONS COORDINATOR FOR THE MASSILLON MUSEUM

ABOUT
- Served as director of the Massillon Museum from 1964 to 1983.
- Became director of the Spring Hill Historic Home following her retirement.
- Led the museum through its first accreditation process.
- Instituted an art education program at the museum.
- Judged art competitions throughout the state.
- Was active member at St. Timothy's Episcopal Church.

STARK CONNECTION
- Grew up in Massillon.
- Headed the Massillon football ticket office.

WILLIAM R. RICHARDSON

"The president of the United States of America, in the name of Congress, takes pleasure in presenting the Congressional Medal of Honor ... for extraordinary heroism in action at Sailor's Creek, Virginia on April 6, 1865."

— PROCLAMATION AWARDING MEDAL OF HONOR

ABOUT
- Born in Cleveland in 1842. Died Oct. 24, 1873
- Member of 2nd Ohio Volunteer Cavalry that fought at the Battle of Sailor's Creek in Virginia on April 6, 1865, in the Civil War.
- Personally recommended by Gen. Phillip Sheridan to receive the Congressional Medal of Honor for bravery.
- Private Richardson was the only survivor of an eight-man recon group sent to investigate the strength and position of Confederate troops; following capture, he escaped and returned to Union lines with information vital to the defeat of enemy forces that day.
- At age 31, he died of illness contracted during the Civil War.

STARK CONNECTION
- After leaving the service, he moved with his wife, Clara, to Massillon, where they raised four children.
- Buried in Massillon City Cemetery with his comrades near the Civil War Soldiers Monument.

HARVEY AKE

"As a jurist, Judge Ake was regarded by the other members of his profession as fair and fearless."

— OBITUARY IN THE CANTON REPOSITORY ON APRIL 20, 1955

ABOUT

- Born Feb. 1, 1872, on a farm near Mapleton. Died April 19, 1955.
- Graduate of Mount Union College and the University of Michigan Law School.
- Admitted to the Ohio and Michigan bars in 1898.
- Served as the 75th grand master of Masons in Ohio from 1931 to 1932.
- Elected delegate to the Republican National Convention in 1924 and helped to nominate Calvin Coolidge.

STARK CONNECTION

- Became the first judge of the Court of Domestic Relations for Stark County in 1929, overseeing domestic issues such as divorce, alimony and custody of minor children for 10 years.
- Elected Stark County Common Pleas Court judge in 1912.
- Retired from the bench in 1935 and returned to private law practice with offices in the Renkert Building in Canton.

JUDITH CARR

ABOUT

- Born Sept. 13, 1938, in New Philadelphia. Died Nov. 19, 2016.
- After her husband, state Rep. Francis Carr, died in 1993, the Ohio House Democratic caucus appointed Carr, a Democrat, to succeed him. She served from 1993 to 1994, when she lost to Republican Ron Hood.
- Elected mayor of Alliance in 1995 and served until 1999, when she lost her bid for re-election to Toni Middleton. She also lost in her attempt to be elected Alliance Municipal Court clerk in 2001. She was appointed to serve as city auditor but lost her bid to keep the job in 2003.
- Helped found Alliance Economic Development Foundation.

STARK CONNECTION

- Graduated from Alliance High School in 1956.
- Administrative assistant to assistant superintendent of Alliance City Schools, Alliance City Schools accountant, Marlington Local Schools accountant and gift shop manager.
- Fourth woman from Stark County to serve in the Ohio General Assembly.
- Got at least three bills passed into law. Signature achievement was legislation making sex between a school employee in a position of authority and a student a felony offense of sexual battery. Also passed bill to allow recreational vehicles to be sold at sports and camping shows; and one to ban baby formula, drugs and cosmetics from being sold at flea markets.

"When I read about this case, I was absolutely shocked. ... Such conduct is clearly improper for a variety of reasons, and it is time we fill this unbelievable gap in Ohio law."

— JUDITH CARR IN AUGUST 1993 ON THE OHIO SUPREME COURT RULING THAT FOUND THAT IT WAS LEGAL FOR AN OTTAWA COUNTY HIGH SCHOOL TEACHER TO HAVE SEX WITH A 16-YEAR-OLD STUDENT.

120

GEORGE MARTIN

"I first met George Martin in 1984 when we were putting together the Los Angeles company of '42nd Street.' He was production stage manager and I was the dance captain. It was the beginning of a strong friendship.

— JON ENGSTROM, ACTORS' EQUITY

ABOUT

- Born Sept. 17, 1924, in Canton; died April 12, 2011, in Atlanta.
- Made his Broadway debut in "Lady in the Dark" in 1942.
- Appeared in "The Waltz King" in 1943. Met wife Ethel in 1944 on the set of "The Yellow Rose of Texas."
- Famous for being a Jack Cole dancer in the 1940s and for being one half of the George and Ethel Martin team.
- On Broadway, danced in productions of "A Funny Thing…," "Donnybrook," "Kismet," "Happy Hunting," "Carnival in Flanders," "Pal Joey," "Magdalena," and "Lady In The Dark."
- In 2004, the Martins retired and donated their papers to Marymount. Among the items are huge theater posters, floor plans, scripts, sheet music and a video collection.

STARK CONNECTION

- Began his dance studies with William Reynolds in Canton.

DAN DIERDORF

"I look at the first couple of plays as being of extra importance. In those first few plays, I try to remove any thought my opponent might have had that that was gonna be his day."

ABOUT

- Born June 29, 1949.
- Played 13 seasons in NFL as an offensive lineman, primarily at tackle. Six-time Pro Bowl pick and member of NFL's 1970s All-Decade team.
- Charter member of Stark County High School Football Hall of Fame in 2002 (Glenwood); College Football Hall of Fame in 2000 (Michigan); and Pro Football Hall of Fame in 1996 (St. Louis Rams).
- Worked as a color analyst for NFL Cardinals before joining ABC's "Monday Night Football" with Al Michaels and Frank Gifford in 1987. He stayed 12 seasons. Also worked games on CBS.
- Works with former Michigan teammate Jim Brandstatter as a color analyst on Michigan football games.

STARK CONNECTION

- For 32 years, held the Stark County shot put record of 60 feet, 8 inches while at Glenwood.
- Worked construction on the building of the original Pro Football Hall of Fame.

JAN RUETZ DeGAETANI

"Miss DeGaetani developed into one of the most respected singers and musicians on the international scene, and in the opinion of many critics, the finest song recitalist that the United States has ever produced. Her creamy voice was wide in range, perfectly placed and produced, always on pitch and handled with consummate artistry."

—NEW YORK TIMES, 1989

ABOUT
- Born June 10, 1933, in Massillon; died Sept. 15, 1989, in Rochester, N.Y.
- Known for her mezzo-soprano performances of contemporary classical vocal compositions.
- Called the "Queen of the avant-garde."
- Performed one of the largest repertoires of any professional singer of her era — ranging from Renaissance music to Cole Porter tunes.

STARK CONNECTION
- Grew up on historic Fourth Street in Massillon.

J. WALTER McCLYMONDS

"Massillon has lost its foremost citizen and the people of our city (have lost) a true and generous friend."

— J.J. WISE, PRESIDENT, MASSILLON BOARD OF TRADE

ABOUT
- Born Sept. 18, 1842, in New Lisbon, OH; died Oct. 5, 1912, in Massillon.
- President of Russell & Co., which manufactured steam engines and farm machinery, shipping them all over the world.
- Founded the Merchants National Bank in Massillon (1890).

STARK CONNECTION
- Built the five-story McClymonds Building (NW corner Erie and Lincoln Way) in downtown Massillon (1909) and the Five Oaks mansion (NE corner Fourth and North) on historic Fourth Street (1894).
- His philanthropy reached throughout the community; his guidance and investment helped countless local businesses and industries.
- With his wife and her family, donated the building for Massillon's first public library, established an endowment fund, and served as president of its initial board of trustees.

REINHARDT AUSMUS

"With minimal education and financial resources, Mr. Ausmus made a distinctive contribution to the progress of early aviation."

— BOB DANIEL, WHO NOMINATED "REINY" FOR THE OHIO VETERANS HALL OF FAME

ABOUT

- Born July 7, 1896, in Cleveland; died Nov. 21, 1970, in Sandusky.
- On the "Roster of Fame" at the Air Force Museum at Dayton.
- Listed as one of the "Early Birds of Aviation," a prestigious group of aviators who piloted prior to Dec. 17, 1916.
- Inducted into the Ohio Veterans Hall of Fame in 2007.
- Flew many missions during World War I, surviving numerous crashes.
- Taught flying lessons until a serious crash in 1922 grounded him.

STARK CONNECTION

- Moved to Massillon as a teenager when he was released from a Cleveland orphanage; lived in the Arlington Hotel on Lincoln Way in downtown Massillon.
- Used nearly all of his income to purchase materials and tools to build an airplane in his hotel room, lowering it to the alley below in two pieces, then assembling it. He first flew June 12, 1912, just outside of Massillon.

RONNIE HARRIS

"I was boxing in the 132-pound division at 5-foot-10, fighting my fights at 115. The Communist countries brought 29- and 30-year-old men in who were professionals. ... It was a thing where you had to be blessed by God, then you had to be in great shape, you had to be tough, you had to have all the skills possible to beat these men."

— HARRIS ON WINNING AN OLYMPIC GOLD MEDAL AFTER GETTING SICK WITH DYSENTERY.

ABOUT

- Born Sept. 3, 1948.
- Boxing gold medalist in the lightweight division at the 1968 Summer Olympics in Mexico City.
- Won three straight AAU lightweight championships from 1966-68.
- Turned pro in 1971, and won his first 28 fights before losing a split decision to Hugo Pastor Corro in 1978 for the WBC-WBA world middleweight title.

STARK CONNECTION

- Graduated from McKinley High School.
- Was taught boxing at the Canton Police Boys Club.
- Won the Novice division at 112 pounds in his first Golden Gloves boxing tournament at Canton Auditorium. Became the Novice champ at 118 a year later.

HENRY "HANK" BULLOUGH

"From Forrest I've learned honesty. His motto is that you can get anything you want out of a player as long as you're willing to do the same things you've asked of him."

— HANK BULLOUGH ABOUT FORREST GREGG, WHOM HE COACHED WITH THE CINCINNATI BENGALS

ABOUT

- Born Jan. 24, 1934, in Scranton, Pa.
- Was a starting guard for Michigan State University, which won the 1954 Rose Bowl.
- Chosen by the Green Bay Packers in the fifth round of the 1955 NFL draft.
- Played for the Packers in 1955 and 1958.
- Assistant coach at Michigan State from 1959 through 1969.
- Coached in NFL for more than two decades as an assistant for Baltimore Colts, New England Patriots, Cincinnati Bengals, Green Bay Packers and Detroit Lions.
- Was co-head coach of New England Patriots and head coach of the Buffalo Bills.
- Enshrined in the Michigan State University Athletics Hall of Fame in 2013.

STARK CONNECTION

- Was All-Ohio as a defensive tackle for Timken High School.
- Was a catcher in Canton Class A baseball.

JUD LOGAN

"He's not a yeller. He's not someone that's going to scream in your face. He's just somebody that when he walks in the room, you respect him. You believe what he says because you know he's been there."

— KURT ROBERTS, ASHLAND UNIVERSITY THROWER, ON HAVING LOGAN AS A COACH

ABOUT

- Born July 19, 1959, in Canton.
- World-class hammer thrower who made four United States Olympic teams (1984, 1988, 1992, 2000).
- Captain on the 1992 U.S. Olympic team.
- Competed at the Pan American Games, Goodwill Games and IAAF World Championships in Athletics.
- Won a gold medal at the 1987 Pan American Games in Indianapolis and a silver medal at the 1991 Pan American Games in Havana, Cuba.
- Held the U.S. record of 268 feet, 8 inches in the hammer throw.

STARK CONNECTION

- Hoover High School graduate.
- Played football at Hoover and at Kent State University. Walked on to the track and field team at Kent State.
- Currently serves as Ashland University's head track and field coach.

PHIL HUBBARD

"I guess I'm a lifer. Basketball has been a big part of my life, and I guess it always will be."

ABOUT
- Won a gold medal playing for the United States men's basketball team in the 1976 Olympics.
- All-American at the University of Michigan, which retired his jersey in 2004.
- Ten-year playing career in the NBA with the Cavaliers and Pistons.
- Has scouted and coached in professional basketball for more than 20 years.

STARK CONNECTION
- Born Dec. 13, 1956, in Canton.
- Grew up on Freedom Avenue in northeast Canton, playing on the courts at Nimisilla Park.
- Still holds record for McKinley's single-season scoring average (25.8).
- McKinley went 48-3 his junior and senior seasons, losing in the state finals and semifinals, respectively.

PAUL V. DeVILLE

"Why should someone leave or slow down from something he likes?"
— PAUL DeVILLE, PRESIDENT, CELEBRATING DeVILLE LUMBER'S 50TH ANNIVERSARY

ABOUT
- Born July 5, 1908, in Canton; died Dec. 3, 2004, in Canton.
- President and founder of DeVille Lumber, which was founded April 1, 1928, at 900 Cleveland Ave. SW as Bartlett Lumber with DeVille as president.
- Purchased land and buildings at 1225 Gross Ave. NE in 1943 to be used as a warehouse. The property became the showroom and building mart in 1955, and offices moved from Cleveland Avenue.
- A fire at the Gross Avenue address in 1969 nearly destroyed the business, but DeVille and his brother, Raymond, decided to rebuild.
- Retired and closed the business in 1987 after 60 years.

STARK CONNECTION
- Lake Cable resident since 1940.
- Past president and director of the Ohio Lumbermen's Association and past president of the National Lumber and Building Material Dealers.
- Served as president of the Lake Cable Recreation Association 19 years.

HARLEY C. PRICE

"One characteristic was dominant throughout his lifetime — sweetness."

— THE CANTON REPOSITORY, OCT. 5, 1964

ABOUT
- Born 1871 in Tallmadge.
- Died 1964 in North Canton at age 93.
- Hoover Co. official for 70 years.

STARK CONNECTION
- Came to New Berlin in 1893 and made saddles for W.H. Hoover Co.
- Became timekeeper, then secretary and chief accountant for W.H. Hoover Co. and Electric Suction Sweeper Co.
- In 1902, wed Mary Catherine Hoover, daughter of William H. "Boss" Hoover.
- Donated funds to build the Hoover-Price Planetarium in Canton and the Hoover-Price Campus Center at the University of Mount Union.

DAVE WOTTLE

"Following the press conference, I was being interviewed by Howard Cosell and Jim McKay. I apologized for leaving it on. They told me not to worry about it."

— DAVE WOTTLE, ON THE HAT HE LEFT ON DURING HIS OLYMPIC GOLD MEDAL CEREMONY

ABOUT
- Born Aug. 7, 1950, in Canton.
- Holds the NCAA record of 3:57.1 for the since-retired mile race
- Running for Bowling Green, won the NCAA outdoor 1,500 meters in 1972 and the NCAA mile in 1973.
- Tied the 800 meters world record (1:44.3) at the 1972 Olympic Trials.
- Outkicked all seven finalists in the last lap to win the 800 meters and the gold medal at the 1972 Olympic Games in Munich, Germany. Stunned by the win, Wottle forgot to remove his trademark golf hat, causing a storm of criticism in America.
- Turned professional in 1974, but retired after a year.
- Served as an administrator for Rhodes College (Tennessee) for 29 years.

STARK CONNECTION
- State champion miler for Lincoln Lions.
- Coached track for Walsh University.

126

MARY REGULA

"Let no one kid you — there is a void in American history."

— MARY REGULA, SPEAKING ABOUT WOMEN DURING A CONVOCATION AT THE UNIVERSITY OF MOUNT UNION

ABOUT
- Founder, president emerita of National First Ladies' Library.
- Convinced Hillary Clinton in 1995 to back the project, after which Clinton became an honorary co-chair.
- Is credited with having the initial idea for a biography of Ida Saxton McKinley.
- Helped dedicate the Lady Bird Johnson postage stamp in 2013.
- Served as president of the Congressional Club, an organization originally started for spouses of members of the U.S. Senate and U.S. House of Representatives.
- Became an inductee of the Ohio Women's Hall of Fame in 1999 in the category of religion and community services.

STARK CONNECTION
- Lives on a 170-acre farm in Bethlehem Township.
- Is a graduate from what is now the University of Mount Union, and earned an honorary doctorate in humanities in 1999 from the university.

HARRY STEEL

"The sixth Buckeye to compete in an Olympics, Harry Dwight Steel became the first Ohio State student athlete to medal and he did so in impressive fashion, winning the gold medal in the heavyweight division at the 1924 Paris Games."

— OHIOSTATEBUCKEYES.COM, "100 BUCKEYES YOU SHOULD KNOW"

ABOUT
- Born April 18, 1899, in East Sparta.
- Died in London in 1971 at age 72.
- Won gold medal in freestyle heavyweight wrestling at the 1924 Paris Olympics as an alternate after placing third in the 1924 AAU tournament. Defeated two-time World Champion Ernst Nilson of Sweden for gold to become the first Ohio State wrestler to earn a gold medal.
- Inducted into Ohio State's Varsity 'O' Hall of Fame in 1980.
- Was the undefeated heavyweight champion of the Western Conference (now Big Ten) as a captain of the 1924 Ohio State wrestling team.
- Helped Ohio State to undefeated wrestling seasons in 1921-1922.
- Lettered for the 1922 and 1923 Ohio State football teams.
- Played on McKinley's 1917 football team.

STARK CONNECTION
- A 1918 McKinley graduate.

127

GARY GRANT

"I played at Canton McKinley High School in Canton, Ohio, and I was a part of the team that won that school's first state title ... I played the point, I directed guys and we ended up having tremendous success. We were the No. 1-ranked team in the country a couple of times in fact. I got my nickname back then, and I took it from there."

ABOUT

- Set assist and steals records at the University of Michigan, where he was chosen Big Ten Player of the Year in 1988.
- A point guard who played 13 seasons in the NBA for four teams: Los Angeles Clippers, New York Knicks, Miami Heat and Portland Trailblazers.
- Drafted 15th overall by Seattle in the first round and traded to Clippers that night.
- Known as "The General," he's remembered most for his days with the Clippers.

STARK CONNECTION

- Born April 21, 1965, in Canton.
- Led McKinley High School to its first state basketball title in 1984.

DR. CLAIR B. KING

"Divine healing is not a substitute for medicine or surgery but is complementary to scientific medicine. Doctors are but instruments in the hands of God."

ABOUT

- Born in Emlenton, Pa.
- Died in Canton in 1986 at age 91.
- General practice doctor, surgeon and eye specialist.
- Graduate of University of Pennsylvania
College of Medicine.

STARK CONNECTION

- Came to Canton in 1924.
- Opened a baby clinic in southwest Canton in 1925.
- Former President of Stark County Medical Society, in which he held the longest continuous membership.
- Founded health ministry at Christ United Presbyterian Church, pictured right, and served as a medical missionary in India.
- Traveled Ohio and other states to give lectures on spiritual healing.

DR. HAROLD JAY BOWMAN

"Dad saved thousands of lives, both in Canton and during the war."

— BETSY SAIMES, DAUGHTER OF DR. HAROLD BOWMAN

ABOUT

- Born Dec. 30, 1909; died Dec. 15, 2001.
- Graduated McKinley High School, College of Wooster, Western Reserve Medical School.
- Served in the Army during World War II, overseas 34 months, from 1942-1945, as chief of surgery and executive officer for the 34th Station Hospital in North Africa and Europe.
- Member of Calvary Presbyterian Church and Brookside Country Club.
- Was a surgeon on staff at Aultman for 44 years, medical staff president in 1960 and chief of surgery 1970 and 1971.
- Was first doctor in Canton to use the Steinmann pin for hips; also first in area to perform a sympathectomy.

STARK CONNECTION

- Served on the boards of Visiting Nurses and YMCA.
- 51-year member of Rotary Club, where he was a Paul Harris Fellow.
- Member of Stark County Medical Association and received its Outstanding Services award.

CHARLEY GRAPEWIN

"Charley Grapewin was best known for his lovable old codger roles in the mid-1900s, like Uncle Henry in 'The Wizard of Oz' and Grandpa Joad in 'The Grapes of Wrath.' "

— MARGY VOGT

ABOUT

- Born Dec. 20, 1869, in Xenia; died Feb. 2, 1956, in Corona, Calif.
- Acted with stock companies onstage and in 109 films.
- His most famous roles were in "The Wizard of Oz" (1939); "The Grapes of Wrath" (1940); "The Petrified Forest" (1936); "The Good Earth" (1937); "They Died with Their Boots On" (1941); and "Tobacco Road" (1941)
- Ran away from home to become a trapeze artist, traveling the world with P.T. Barnum.
- Appeared in the 1903 Broadway production of "The Wizard of Oz," 35 years before his role in the film version.
- A street is named for him in Corona, Calif., where he lived at the end of his life.

STARK CONNECTION

- Spend his boyhood in Massillon, where his father owned the Hotel Massillon, near the Pennsylvania Railroad depot.

129

CHARLEY STANCEU

"Tom Brokaw dubbed Americans who lived through the Depression and served in World War II 'The Greatest Generation.' As a member of this group, Charley Stanceu found himself witnessing some of the iconic events of that period.

— CHRIS RAINEY, HISTORIAN

ABOUT

- Born Jan. 9, 1916, in Canton; died April 3, 1969, in Canton.
- Went 3-3 with a 5.63 ERA in 22 games for the World Series-winning New York Yankees in 1941, becoming the first major leaguer of Romanian descent.
- Joined the Army in January 1942 and fought in the "Battle of the Bulge," eventually earning a Bronze Star.
- Pitched for the Yankees and Philadelphia Phillies in 1946, finishing his career with a 5-7 record and a 4.93 ERA.

STARK CONNECTION

- Attended McKinley High School, although he did not graduate with his 1934 class.
- Played in Canton's Class B league, signing with the minor league Zanesville Greys in 1934 after tossing a no-hitter that impressed the team's manager.
- Worked at Hartville's Monarch Rubber Co. after his playing career.

JAMES SECCOMBE

"First steps in a movement to cut down the number of left turns in the business district and probably to eliminate them all eventually will be taken by an order directing buses to make no left turns in the public square."

— THE EVENING REPOSITORY ON AUG. 9, 1930, QUOTING COUNCILMAN JAMES SECCOMBE.

ABOUT

- Born Feb. 12, 1893, in Mineral City.
- Moved to Canton in 1906.
- Served in the U.S. Army during World War I, from 1917 to 1919.
- Died Aug. 23, 1970, in Canton.

STARK CONNECTION

- Served on Canton City Council and as mayor between 1932 and 1933. Again elected mayor and served from 1936 until his resignation in 1938.
- Represented Ohio's 16th Congressional District between 1939 and 1941.
- Later worked as a state tax examiner in Canton and then as director of the Stark County Board of Elections.

BOB "FATS" FOTHERGILL

"He was one of the last of those rare spirits who appeared to play for the fun of it. After the game, you could find him with a thick porterhouse steak and a seidel of beer, and he would chuckle to himself, 'Imagine getting paid for a life like this!' "

— AUTHOR LEE ALLEN, THE COMPLETEARMCHAIR BOOK OF BASEBALL

ABOUT

- Born Aug. 16, 1897, in Massillon. Died March 20, 1938, in Detroit.
- Became one of the best contact hitters in Major League Baseball history, with a batting average of .325. Ranks 37th all-time, just behind Honus Wagner and just ahead of Joe DiMaggio. Not in Hall of Fame because he averaged just 92 games across his 12-year career.
- Nicknamed "Fatty" then "Fats" then "Fat," based on eventually carrying as much as 240 pounds on a 5-foot-11 frame. Surprised fans with his nimbleness and speed.
- Once ended a home-run trot by doing a complete flip, ending with his feet on home plate.
- His appearance and production led to another nickname — "The People's Choice" — while he was hitting .337 across nine seasons (1922-30) with the Tigers.

STARK CONNECTION

- Grew up in Massillon and played pro football for the Massillon Tigers and Canton Bulldogs. Was still living in Massillon, working as a blacksmith, when he signed his first pro baseball contract at age 23.
- When he died at age 40, was survived by his wife and four sisters and was buried in Massillon.

ANTHONY BLAIR

"When you think of all the great University of Tennessee track athletes that program has produced, stars such as Willie Gault and countless others, it doesn't get much better than to be in their prestigious HOF."

— ALLIANCE REVIEW, APRIL 14, 2016

ABOUT

- Attended Alliance High School from 1975-78.
- Attended University of Tennessee from 1978-81.
- Blair is one of the greatest sprinters in area track and field history.
- Blair went on to be a star at University of Tennessee, winning two NCAA Division I National Championships as part of relay teams. He was inducted into the first University of Tennessee Athletics Hall of Fame class in 2016.
- Blair made the United States Olympic Team as part of the 1,600-meter relay in 1980, but the boycott prevented his participation.

STARK CONNECTION

- He won three state titles at Alliance High School in the 440-yard dash in his career.
- Blair still holds the Stark County record in the 200 meters (20.8) and 400 meters (46.5).

DON SCOTT

ABOUT

- Died Oct. 1, 1943.
- Scott is one of the most decorated and recognized football players in Stark County history.
- Scott's versatility and outstanding play caught the eye of Ohio State. He went on to letter three years, leading the Buckeyes to a Big Ten title in his first year as a starter as a junior. He would go on to earn All-American honors for his play as a junior and a senior.
- Scott was highly sought after by NFL teams after graduation. He was the ninth pick overall by the Chicago Bears in 1941.
- Decided to forego an immediate NFL career and enlisted as a pilot in the Air Force.
- Scott unfortunately never would get the opportunity to suit up for Chicago. He was killed when his plane crashed in England on Oct. 1, 1943, during a training exercise.

STARK CONNECTIONS

- He was selected all-state twice. As a sophomore, Scott started along the offensive and defensive lines at McKinley High School in the 1930s. Scott also served as a punter and a kicker for the Bulldogs. Scott moved to quarterback and halfback his junior and senior years. With Scott leading the way, the Bulldogs reached the state semifinals twice.
- The McKinley football field as well as the Ohio State airport were subsequently renamed Don Scott Field after the tragedy.

"In honor of Scott, exactly one month after his passing, a vote by Ohio State's board of trustees christened the school's recently opened airport as Don Scott Field."
— TRIBUTE PAGE AT ELEVENWARRIORS.COM

C. GILBERT TAYLOR

"Self-taught aircraft designer whose Taylor Cub evolved into the overwhelmingly successful Piper Cub of the 1930s and 1940s."

— FROM HIS OBITUARY THAT APPEARED IN THE NEW YORK TIMES ON APRIL 12, 1988

ABOUT

- Born Sept. 25, 1898; died March 29, 1988.
- Considered a founding father of private aviation.
- Designed his first airplane as a teenager, in his family's attic in Rochester, N.Y.
- In 1928, went to Bradford, Pa., to produce the Taylor Brothers two-seat Chummy airplane with financial backing from William Piper.
- After Taylor and Piper parted ways in 1935, Taylor landed near Alliance.

STARK CONNECTION

- In 1935, moved into the former Hess-Argo airfield and hangar, north of Alliance. Taylorcraft Aviation Corp., with help from the Alliance Chamber of Commerce, brought equipment and employees from Bradford, Pa. In its heyday, Taylorcraft employed more than 750 people.
- The company constructed runways, which still are visible today, and began producing a two-seat Taylorcraft airplane.
- Bankruptcy ultimately halted production here in 1948.
- The company changed hands over the years and exists today as Taylorcraft, based in Brownsville, Texas.

JOHN B. BARKER

"They enthusiastically wanted him to stay, and he equally as enthusiastically cast aside other pulpit calls so that he could stay. Only death could take him away, as it did Sunday."

— EDITORIAL IN THE CANTON REPOSITORY ON SEPT. 5, 1967

ABOUT

- Took over as pastor of Calvary Presbyterian Church in Canton in April 21, 1929, and saw the church's membership grow from 212 to more than 2,300 over his 38-year career.
- Served as president of the Urban League.
- Died Sept. 3, 1967, at age 68.

STARK CONNECTION

- Namesake of the John Barker Springhouse (right), a brick-pillared building built in 1968 along Monument Drive NW near Stadium Park, where fresh water runs 24 hours a day. The city of Canton maintains the springhouse.

JOHN H. LEHMAN

"Being the first to do anything is difficult. Mr. Lehman was the superintendent trailblazer for Canton. The result of his work is a well respected education system, and many Cantonians who are proud graduates of Lehman High School."

— ADRIAN E. ALLISON, SUPERINTENDENT, CANTON CITY SCHOOLS

ABOUT

- Born in 1846 in Lancaster, Pa.
- Came to Ohio with his family in 1859, first to Wayne County, then to Stark.

STARK CONNECTION

- Canton's first superintendent of schools; served 12 years, from 1876 to 1888.

- Served on the Board of Education from 1902 to 1916 and as president for 12 years.
- Authored a three volume Standard History of Stark County, Ohio.

MAJ. AUGUSTUS VIGNOS

Upon returning from a trip to Mexico, where the one-armed veteran engaged in mountain climbing, while his daughter went ballooning: "Mountain-climbing is ten-fold more dangerous than this balloon sport," he told The Repository in a 1909 story.

ABOUT

- Born Sept. 16, 1838, in Louisville; died July 22, 1926, in Los Angeles, Calif.
- Served in the Union 107th Ohio Volunteer Infantry during the Civil War.
- Fought in the Civil War's Battle of Gettysburg, where he lost his right arm to a cannonball.
- Confederate soldiers left him for dead on the battlefield.
- Returned to battle with his regiment, even after losing his arm, refusing to be qualified as disabled.

STARK CONNECTION

- Served as Canton postmaster.
- Founded Novelty Cutlery Co. in Canton, selling personalized pocket knives.
- President of American Mine Door Co.

GEORGE L. DEAL

"My father, W.R. Timken, had the highest confidence and trust in George. He was my father's right-hand man and very often was his personal representative to the community."

— W.R. "TIM" TIMKEN JR., FORMER TIMKEN CO. CHAIRMAN AND U.S. AMBASSADOR TO GERMANY, DISCUSSING DEAL IN 2002.

ABOUT

- Joined Timken Co. in 1936 and became treasurer in 1953, secretary-treasurer in 1955 and vice president of finance in 1964.
- He served as a company director from 1960 until 1976, two years after his retirement.
- Received the Canton Regional Chamber of Commerce Award of Merit in 1973.
- Helped direct finances for the United Way of Central Stark County and the McKinley Museum, and a co-founder of Canton Country Day School.
- Served 46 years as a member of the Stark County Historical Society.

STARK CONNECTION

- Born in Canton on Sept. 5, 1914, and lived his whole life in the community. Died Jan. 19, 2002.

ROBERT A. POLLOCK

"Sen. Pollock made many notable contributions to Ohio's welfare during his years in the assembly. He introduced the first mine safety legislation, was a pioneer in school consolidation and pupil transportation movements … and was the author of several workmen's compensation laws."

— EDITORIAL IN THE REPOSITORY ON NOV. 15, 1956

ABOUT

- Born Aug. 24, 1870 in North Lawrence; died Nov. 13, 1956.
- In 1899, elected as a Republican to the state Legislature.
- Represented Stark County for 13 terms, known as the "dean of Ohio legislators."
- Introduced a bill to fly the American flag over schools and to teach patriotism. Created legislation resulting in what would become Canton Municipal Court.

STARK CONNECTION

- Got his start in politics driving a horse and buggy for his idol, William McKinley.
- Worked starting at age 12 at a coal mine in Massillon; as rail mail clerk; operated a mercantile business with his father in North Lawrence; and served as postmaster and justice of the peace for North Lawrence.

ANGELO ARGEA

"Angelo always went out early in the morning and got the pins, and knew enough of the golf course, and my golf game, that any information I needed, he generally had. But it's as important, or more important, that the player and the caddie have compatible personalities. Angelo and I always had a very good rapport."

— JACK NICKLAUS SHORTLY AFTER ARGEA'S DEATH

ABOUT

- Born Nov. 27, 1929, in Greece.
- Died Oct. 10, 2005, in Canton.
- Primary caddy for Jack Nicklaus during the prime of the golf legend's career.
- Was a Las Vegas taxi driver in early 1960s when he had someone tell Nicklaus before a PGA Tour stop that Argea was the caddy assigned to him. An amused Nicklaus, knowing caddies were not assigned for that event, decided to give Argea a try. They hit it off quickly, and Nicklaus won five of their first six tournaments together.
- Wrote "The Bear and I: The Story of the World's Most Famous Caddy," in 1979.
- Last "major" win with Nicklaus was at 1980 U.S. Open at Baltusrol.
- Member of the National Caddies Hall of Fame.

STARK CONNECTION

- Grew up in and spent much of his life in Canton.

DR. LEWIS SLUSSER

"About the bedside of the dying man were the sorrowing members of the family. ... The death will be a great shock to hundreds in Canton and vicinity."

— FROM THE FRONT-PAGE DEATH NOTICE OF DR. LEWIS SLUSSER, PUBLISHED DEC. 23, 1892, IN THE EVENING REPOSITORY.

ABOUT

- Born Jan. 21, 1820; died Dec. 23, 1892.
- Civil War veteran and surgeon in Stark County.
- Served three terms in the Ohio House of Representatives.
- Practiced medicine in Cleveland before returning to Canton.
- An author and historian who wrote a detailed history of townships in Stark County.
- An unfailing advocate of the mentally ill and for seeking state and national standards for surgeons.

STARK CONNECTION

- Born on a farm within corporate limits of Canton to John Slusser and Nancy DeWalt. Member of one of the oldest families in Stark County.

AL MEYER

"I wish that I would have known him, he was so well liked."

— MEYER'S SON, A.V. MEYER, IN "A HISTORY OF EARLY STARK COUNTY AVIATION" BY ROBERT L. BURWELL.

ABOUT

- Died Aug. 19, 1934.
- Flight instructor and barnstorming stunt pilot from Massillon.
- Owned a gas station at 845 Tremont St.
- Founded an airport in Massillon at Cherry Hill on Cherry Road.
- Had a reputation as a capable and careful pilot.
- He and a flight student fell to their deaths from a stalled plane while flying upside down.
- Incident reported in the May 1936 edition of Popular Science magazine.

STARK CONNECTION

- Lived on Walnut Road in Massillon.
- Had a wife who was pregnant and gave birth to a son, A.V. Meyer, a few months after Meyer's death.

136

C.J. RODMAN

"His contributions to the community will be serving citizens for many years, which is a tribute to his foresight, generosity and belief in present and future of Alliance."

— REPOSITORY EDITORIAL, FEB. 1, 1972.

ABOUT

- Born in Milwaukee in 1890. Died Jan. 30, 1972, in Alliance.
- Industrialist and inventor who developed nonmetal propellers for airplanes during World War I and submarine-seeking torpedoes during World War II.
- In 1934, founded Alliance Ware Inc. (originally the Alliance Porcelain Products Co.), a leader in porcelain enameled sinks, toilets, bathtubs and other products.
- A partner in the Alliance Manufacturing Co. A prolific businessman, he also founded the Steel Sanitary Co. and Alliance Tool Co.
- Served on the Alliance Board of Education, was director of two Alliance banks and a leader of local development corporations; member of the Rotary Club, Wrangler's Club, Exchange Club and Freemasons.

STARK CONNECTION

- In 1963, pledged $250,000 to build a new library in Alliance if the community would match his donation. Rodman Public Library is named in his honor.

C.J. McCOLLUM

"Being raised in Canton, Ohio, making it to this stage, it means a lot to me."

— McCOLLUM, AT HIS MOST IMPROVED PLAYER NEWS CONFERENCE, 2016

ABOUT

- NBA Most Improved Player, 2016.
- Averaged 20.8 points, the highest single-season average by a Stark County native in the NBA.
- Lottery pick (10th overall) by the Trail Blazers in the 2013 NBA Draft.
- All-American college career at Lehigh University included upset of Duke in the NCAA Tournament.
- Gatorade Ohio Player of the Year as a senior at GlenOak High School.

STARK CONNECTION

- Born Sept. 19, 1991, in Canton to Errick and Kathy McCollum.
- Graduated from GlenOak in 2009 as the school's all-time leading scorer (1,405).
- Older brother Errick II is successful pro basketball player overseas.

DON DIXON

"Songwriting is spotty for me. I don't write like some of my Nashville friends who sit down and put in work every day like a 9-to-5 job. I'm very project oriented. ... And I sweat over every word. The more spontaneous it sounds, the harder I had to work."

ABOUT

- Born Dec. 13, 1950, in Lancaster, S.C.
- Former resident of Chapel Hill, N.C.
- Dixon and Mitch Easter co-produced R.E.M.'s critically acclaimed album "Murmur" in 1983; the record was named Rolling Stone Magazine's best album that year over Michael Jackson's "Thriller" and U2's "War." He also co-produced R.E.M.'s follow-up, "Reckoning."
- Produced albums for the Smithereens and his wife, Marti Jones, among many other artists.
- Accomplished singer-songwriter and musician who has released more than 20 solo albums, including two duet recordings with his wife; his songs have been recorded by Joe Cocker, Counting Crows, Ronnie Spector, Hootie & the Blowfish and other artists.
- Touring as bass player for Mary Chapin Carpenter. In 2016, he released a six-song collection, "I Lived in the Time of Organ Grinders."
- Producing records for the Gin Blossoms, Chris Allen, David Childers and John Rooney as well as one for the West Virginia Music Hall of Fame featuring Bill Withers, Kathy Mattea and others.

STARK CONNECTION

- Moved to Canton in 1988.
- Dixon's wife is originally from Uniontown.

THELMA E. SLATER

"I have retired from the Canton City Schools twice. In 1981, I retired from a full-time position as a guidance counselor and certified teacher. In 2006, I retired from my part-time position as both teacher and counselor in Canton's adult education program. Throughout all my years as a salaried employee, however, I also served as a literacy volunteer."

ABOUT

- Born June 21, 1921; died Nov. 24, 2013.
- Educator and literacy advocate.
- Graduate of Washington High School in Massillon; earned teaching degree at what then was Mount Union College; earned master's degree in education at Kent State University.
- Worked as a teacher and counselor for Canton City Schools for 59 years and initiated the first elementary school counseling program.
- Received the Lifetime Achievement Award of Stark County Teachers Association, Washington High School Distinguished Citizen Award and was Outstanding Teacher for Canton City Schools.

STARK CONNECTION

- Taught hundreds of children and adults in Stark County how to read.
- Helped organize the Mayor's Literacy Commission and for years spearheaded the annual One Book, One Community program.

J. TED WENGER

"I was just so happy with my job. I couldn't believe I got paid for doing what I loved, and I was so proud of all the students that became music teachers."

ABOUT

- Born March 31, 1937.
- Perry High School band director from about 1966 to 1995, after teaching four years each at Sandy Valley and Canton South high schools.
- School Band of America Jazz Band director during 1975 European tour.
- Graduated from Kent State University with a degree in music education in 1959 and earned a master's degree from Vander Cook College of Music in 1972.
- Enshrined in Ohio Band Directors Hall of Fame in 2002.

STARK CONNECTION

- Resides in Jackson Township.
- Graduated from Canton South High School in 1955.
- Adjunct music instructor at University of Mount Union from about 1997-2007.
- Director of Stark County Fair Band at least 10 years, ending in 2013.

LOU MARINI

"The hipness level goes up the minute he walks in the room and it goes through the roof whenever he plays."

— MAUREEN McGOVERN, VOCALIST, ACTRESS AND SONGWRITER.

ABOUT

- Born in 1945 in Charleston, S.C.
- Graduated from Fairless High School, where his father, Lou Marini Sr., was band director.
- Saxophone, flute and clarinet player, as well as arranger, composer, producer and educator.
- Played in the Woody Herman Orchestra; house band for "Saturday Night Live"; Blood, Sweat and Tears; The Band; Tonight Show Band; David Letterman Show House Band; and with Maureen McGovern, Eric Clapton and Frank Zappa. Currently playing in James Taylor's and Linda Carter's touring bands.
- Acted and played sax in both Blues Brothers movies, with his "Blue Lou" nickname given to him by actor Dan Aykroyd.

STARK CONNECTION

- Inducted into Fairless High School Alumni Association Hall of Honor.
- Beach City resident.

THOMAS S. FARRELL

"If one of the outcomes of my years of activity as an educator with spiritual and religious motivations is that people have become better and more highly motivated, then the result has been good."

— FARRELL IN AN INTERVIEW IN 1987 WITH THE REPOSITORY.

ABOUT

- Born Dec. 17, 1911, in Montreal.
- Died Oct. 8, 1988, in Canton.
- Joined the order Brothers of Christian Instruction in La Prairie, Quebec, in 1927 and made his final vows to become a Catholic priest in 1933.
- Bachelor and masters degrees from St. Michael's College and did graduate studies at University of Montreal, Highlands College in England and Catholic University in Washington, D.C.
- Served as assistant director of Catholic Charities for the Diocese of Youngstown from 1970-77.

STARK CONNECTION

- The first president and one of the seven founders of Walsh College in North Canton, which opened in 1960. Retired as college president in 1970.
- Returned to Walsh in 1977 as special assistant to its president. Served on board of trustees until he died; named president emeritus in 1985.

VICTORIA CLAFLIN WOODHULL

"While others prayed for the good time coming, I worked for it."

ABOUT

- Born Sept. 23, 1838, Homer, Ohio; died June 9, 1927, Bredon, United Kingdom.
- First female candidate for president of the United States, 1872, decades before women had the right to vote.
- Prominent national women's rights activist and lecturer.
- First female to testify before a congressional committee.
- She and her sister, Tennessee, served as first female stock brokers on Wall Street.
- President of the National Spiritualist Association.

STARK CONNECTION

- Lived on Federal Avenue NE in Massillon with her family as a young woman.

BISHOP JOHN MICHAEL BOTEAN

"We have a mission to the church, and therefore the whole world, because we speak our faith in our language. We experience it through our life. Our way of looking at the world is different."

ABOUT
- Graduate of Oakwood High School, St. Fidelis Seminary, the Catholic University of America; St. Gregory's Melkite Seminary, Holy Cross Greek Orthodox School of Theology, Catholic Theological Union.
- Ordained in 1986; elevated to bishop in 1996.
- Vicar General, Apostolic Administrator, 1993-1996.
- Rector, St. George Cathedral, Canton, 1990-1993.
- Pastor, Aurora, Ill., 1986-1990.
- Staff member, Pax Christi USA Center on Conscience and War, Cambridge, Mass. Administrative assistant, Center for Applied Research in the Apostolate (CARA), Washington, D.C.

STARK CONNECTION
- Prelate of the Romanian Catholic Diocese Eparchy of St. George the Martyr, Canton.
- Born July 9, 1955, in Canton.
- Canton Repository Teen of the Year, 1973.

THE REV. P.H. WELSHIMER

"It has been thrilling work all the way through ... It has been a happy work."

ABOUT
- Born April 6, 1873, in York, Ohio.
- Died Aug. 16, 1957.
- Graduate, Ohio Northern University, 1894; Hiram College, 1897; doctorates from Cincinnati Bible Seminary, Butler University and Milligan College, home of the P.H. Welshimer Memorial Library.
- First pastoral assignment, Millersburg Christian Church, 1897.
- Founded Phillips Bible Institute, 1912.

STARK CONNECTION
- Pastor, First Christian Church in Canton, 1902 to 1956. A new church was built in 1905, adding 606 new members. Another church was built in 1921, when 345 people joined. In the 1950s, First Christian had 6,000 members, with one of largest Sunday schools in the United States.

HARRY JOHNS

"Be not worried for in due season, you will reap if you fret not."

— HARRY JOHNS' FAVORITE QUOTE

ABOUT

- Born Dec. 7, 1921.
- Volunteered to serve in Army in 1940.
- Graduated from Wilberforce College with a bachelor of science degree in accounting in 1947.
- Received a master of arts degree from Columbia University in 1949.
- Hired in 1949 as bursar at Central State University, where a scholarship is named for him.
- Was named vice president of physical affairs and director of physical and future planning at Central State in 1959.
- Was named first black president of Xenia Rotary Club in 1974.

STARK CONNECTION

- Born in Alliance to Iona Huskey Johns and Ewing James.
- Graduated from Alliance High School in 1939.

MARSHALL B. BELDEN SR.

"Golly. This all starts with the passion of the museum's founder, Marshall Belden Sr., who ran an oil business in Canton, and also collected cars."

— PROFILE OF CANTON CLASSIC CAR MUSEUM ON HEMMINGS.COM.

ABOUT

- Born: 1912.
- Died: 1995.
- A businessman and preservationist, he was founder of Belden & Blake Co.
- He served as board chair for MB Operating Co.
- Co-founder, Canton Classic Car Museum.
- Spearheaded the restoration of several historic structures in downtown Canton, including the Saxton-Barber House, now the First Ladies Library; the Eagles Building; and the Schuffeneker Apartments.

STARK CONNECTION

- Great-nephew of President William McKinley and great-great-grandson of Canton Repository founder John Saxton.

HERBERT ROSENGARD

"It is very rare that you return to a former location in JCC (Jewish Community Center), but they invited me back in 1963 as assistant executive director."

ABOUT

- Born Aug. 2, 1927, in Chicago.
- Died Feb. 3, 2010, at Bethany Nursing Home.
- Graduated from University of Illinois in 1948; he was varsity football, baseball letterman.
- Played baseball in St. Louis Cardinals farm system.

STARK CONNECTION

- After college, he started his career as physical education instructor at the Canton Jewish Community Center in 1953.
- Became assistant director of the center in 1963; was executive director from 1967-87.
- Active in Pro Football Hall of Fame Enshrinement festivities — head of security, chairman of Balloon Festival.
- Became manager of Arrowhead Country Club in 1988.

DR. J.B. WALKER

"They were hard workers, and they taught us to love the Lord."

— THE REPOSITORY, FEB. 26, 2012

ABOUT

- Born in 1889 in Heathsville, Va.
- Died in 1995.
- Graduate, Howard University, and Howard Medical College.

STARK CONNECTION

- Became Canton's first black physician in 1920.
- Opened his medical practice on Cherry Street SE in Canton.
- Helped to organize the Canton Urban League in 1921.
- Served on a number of civic boards, including the Canton Board of Health, Canton YMCA, Malone College, Canton Welfare Federation, Stark and Canton Tuberculosis Health committees; chairman, Christma Seals.

143

ELIZABETH "MOLLY" PAGE STARK

"There are your enemies, the Redcoats and the Tories. They are ours, or this night Molly Stark sleeps a widow!"
— JOHN STARK, AS HE LED 1,200 TROOPS INTO THE BATTLE OF BENNINGTON, AMERICAN REVOLUTIONARY WAR

ABOUT
- Born Feb. 16, 1737, in Haverhill, Mass.
- Married Aug. 20, 1758, to John Stark, American Revolutionary War general. The couple had 11 children.
- Died June 29, 1814, of typhus.

STARK CONNECTION
- Wife of the man for whom Stark County is named.
- The Daughters of the American Revolution named a chapter after her.
- Served as nurse to her husband's troops during smallpox epidemic, and opened their home in Vermont as a hospital during the war. Molly Stark Sanatorium was opened Aug. 23, 1929, in her name. The hospital was opened to care for Stark County residents suffering from tuberculosis. By 1956, it serviced those needing physical rehabilitation, suffering drug and alcohol abuse issues and having problems related to aging. The hospital closed in 1995.
- A statue erected in Southern Vermont marks the Molly Stark Trail. It's the route her husband used to make his victory march from battle in 1777.

DR. HYMIE GINSBURG

"A prominent member of Canton's Jewish community, Ginsburg felt that mixing religions (Walsh was established by the Roman Catholic Church) and athletics was 'good for brotherhood.' "
— BEAVER COUNTY (PA.) SPORTS HALL OF FAME"

ABOUT
- Born March 23, 1914.
- Died March 2, 1986 in Canton.
- Played basketball at Beaver Falls High School in Pennsylvania, Geneva College and for the Pittsburgh Pirates in the National Basketball League.
- Inducted into the Beaver County Sports Hall of Fame in 2010.

STARK CONNECTION
- Established the men's basketball program at Walsh University.
- Compiled a 24-34 record in four seasons as head coach of the Cavaliers.
- Inducted into the Walsh University Wall of Fame in 1988.
- Set up a thriving practice in Stark County after becoming a dentist.

OLGA T. WEBER

ABOUT

- Born April 27, 1903. Died Aug. 1, 1978.
- In 1951, Weber distributed copies of the Constitution, Bill of Rights, flag booklets and patriotic leaflets to local schools, churches, libraries and the public.
- In 1952, she petitioned Louisville leaders to establish Constitution Day in honor of the signing of the U.S. Constitution in 1787. Sept. 17 was declared Constitution Day in the city.
- In 1953, her efforts led to the Ohio General Assembly proclaiming Sept. 17 as statewide Constitution Day. That year, she urged the U.S. Congress to declare Sept. 17-23 as Constitution Week. In 1955, President Dwight D. Eisenhower designated Constitution Week.
- On April 15, 1957, Louisville City Council declared the city Constitution Town.

"In 1951, Mrs. Olga T. Weber, a mother and homemaker, fearing that we were taking our freedoms too much for granted, resolved to do something about it."

— LOUISVILLE PUBLIC LIBRARY'S WEBSITE

STARK CONNECTION

- Weber's efforts led to the city of Louisville annually holding a Constitution Week festival that includes a queen's pageant, car show, balloon liftoffs, choir concert, community banquet, prayer breakfast, fireworks and parade.
- Historical markers designating Louisville as Constitution Town were placed at the four main entrances to town in 1958.

FRANK E. CASE

"The sincere sorrow felt for his death is lightened only by his good fortune in having been able to live so long."

— FEB. 8, 1933, REPOSITORY EDITORIAL ABOUT THE DEATH OF FRANK E. CASE.

ABOUT

- Born on a farm in Ashland. Came to Stark County to practice law.
- At various times a farmer, educator, lawyer, inventor, banker, real-estate developer and businessman.
- In 1887, invented the first reclining dental chair. Went on to hold numerous other patents.
- After manufacturing dental chairs in his basement, founded the successful Harvard Dental Manufacturing Co. At one point, a third of all dental offices in the country had furniture from the company.
- An avid art collector who became a painter in his 70s.
- Died Feb. 6, 1933.

STARK CONNECTION

- Bequeathed his home and extensive art collection to Canton. The gift later became the Canton Art Institute, the city's first art museum and a predecessor of the Canton Museum of Art.

CONRAD BRUMBAUGH

"Shortly after 1803, when Ohio was admitted to the Union, Conrad Brumbaugh laid claim to a significant amount of land boarding the eastern shore of Congress Lake."

— THE HERITAGE OF CONGRESS LAKE CLUB RECORD

ABOUT

- Born May 29, 1768, in Maryland.
- Died Dec. 6, 1859.
- Settled the land that today is Quail Hollow Park, building there around 1820.
- Served in Revolutionary War.
- Used a tomahawk to clear a path from Middlebranch to what is now Hartville on hunting expeditions.
- His family operated a sawmill on the southern border of Congress Lake.
- Built a 24-foot by 24-foot, two-story log cabin with a stone basement.

STARK CONNECTION

- One of Stark County's first settlers, arriving in 1807.
- Farmed the land that became Congress Lake golf course.

DARRELL C. ROMICK

An article in the May 1956 edition of Popular Science outlined Romick's plans for a 3,000-foot-long space station powered by solar panels and equipped with laboratories, telescopes, vehicle docking areas and living quarters for 20,000 people.

ABOUT

- During the 1950s, he was a member of the American Rocket Society's spaceflight committee and presented papers that suggested a future with rockets using ion propulsion, reusable launch vehicles, permanently occupied space stations and manned moon missions.
- Worked as an aero physicist for Goodyear Tire & Rubber Co. in the aerospace division, retiring in 1977 after more than 30 years.
- While at Goodyear he also worked with the Army's guided missile project and developed Project METEOR, which had a key role in development of the space shuttle.
- Earned a bachelor's degree in engineering physics from the University of Illinois.
- Member of the International Astronautical Federation and the American Rocket Society.
- Born March 4, 1915, in Adair, Iowa. Died May 13, 2008, in Stark County.

STARK CONNECTION

- Lived more than 50 years in North Canton in a house he built.

146

ERNEST NICKLES

"He was still trying to learn more about how to make the bakery better," said nephew David A. Gardner in a 2013 interview with The Repository, in explaining why the 87-year-old Ernest Nickles spent two hours discussing the family business with a Bakery wholesale salesman in January 1995. The next day, Nickles suffered a stroke that led to his death.

ABOUT
- Born Oct. 1, 1907. Died Feb. 28, 1995, in Stark County.
- Son of Alfred Nickles, founder of Nickles Bakery in Navarre.
- Inducted into American Society of Baking's Baking Hall of Fame in 2013.

STARK CONNECTION
- Began working for Nickles Bakery in 1925.
- Worked for the business for 70 years.
- Succeeded his father as president and chief executive after father's death in 1949.
- Transformed the bakery from a home-route to a wholesale business.
- Worked seven days a week, walking to the Navarre plant one block from his home.

FRANK TRANSUE

"The eventual success of these experiments was probably the greatest single event in Stark County history, making the county the greatest center of electric-furnace alloy steel production in the world."

— FROM "THE STARK COUNTY STORY," BY HISTORIAN E.T. HEALD

ABOUT
- Born June 17, 1842, in North Benton.
- Died April 29, 1925, in Alliance.
- His estate was valued at almost $600,000 at time of his death.

STARK CONNECTION
- With Silas Williams, formed the Transue-Williams Steel Forging Corp. in 1895.

- Company employed 1,700 people in its heyday.
- Placed on Stark County Wall of Fame in 2003.
- His forging company was instrumental in Henry Ford's plan for assembly-line auto production.
- Henry Ford was able to get lightweight steel made at United Steel in Canton, which was then forged at Transue-Williams.

SAMMY ANGOTT

"A game and willing fighter, unafraid to fight everyone from featherweights to welterweights, Sammy Angott proved one of the toughest customers in boxing."

— NATIONAL ITALIAN AMERICAN SPORTS HALL OF FAME

ABOUT

- Born Jan. 17, 1915, in Washington, Pa. Died Oct. 22, 1980.
- Three-time world lightweight boxing champion.
- Won the vacant National Boxing Association lightweight title when he defeated Davey Day in a 15-round decision in May 1940. In December 1941, defeated Lew Jenkins at Madison Square Garden in a 15-round decision to become the undisputed world lightweight champion.
- Earned the nickname "The Clutch" for grabbing his opponent following clean punches Angott landed. Described as a clever fighter who used a stinging jab and fast, hard hooks to wear down opponents.
- Inducted into The Ring magazine's boxing Hall of Fame and the International Boxing Hall of Fame.

STARK CONNECTION

- Following retirement from boxing, Angott lived in Massillon more than 20 years.
- Worked at Eaton, Yale & Towne in Massillon; retired due to severe arthritis in his hips and joints.
- Worked with young boys and developmentally disabled children at Canton Police Boys Club.

JACOB SCHWARTZ

Schwartz was "a prominent promoter of the agricultural interests of the county."

— EXCERPT FROM A "HISTORY OF STARK COUNTY"

ABOUT

- A prominent livestock breeder and farmer.
- Won first place for cattle in 1889 at the Stark County Fair.
- His family, which remains active in the fair and was the first family to have three members on the fair board at the same time, dropped the "ch" in their name about 1900.

STARK CONNECTION

- Co-founded and directed the Stark County Agricultural Society.
- Helped plan the county's first fair in October 1850.
- His family's role in agriculture is included in a "History of Stark County" book.

RICHARD "DICK" BARNARD

"The youth are not the church's future; they are a part of the present church. The church has to be sensitive to their needs with a program that speaks to the validity of their faith. Adults don't think the youth are capable of taking part in the church. And sometimes, they're scared by the exuberance of youth."

ABOUT

- Nicknamed "The Beam" for the flashlight he carried at Christ Presbyterian's Camp Wakonda.
- Served 41 years as youth director at Christ Presbyterian Church, retiring in 1993 at age 65.
- Led mission trips to places such as Pine Ridge Indian Reservation in South Dakota and France.

STARK CONNECTION

- A native of Alliance.
- Died at age 84 in 2012 in Canton.

SISTER COLETTA BAST

"Being a nun is what I've always to wanted be. This was my calling."

ABOUT

- Catholic educator and member of the Sisters of the Humility of Mary. Her religious name was Sister Marie José.
- Born in 1921 in Canton. Died Oct. 8, 2003.
- Graduate of St. John's Catholic School, 1939; entered Villa Maria Convent, 1940; missionary in Temuco, Chile, 1963, and Cleveland's Latino community; principal of St. Sebastian School, Akron; returned to St. John's in 1981. Retired to Villa Maria.

STARK CONNECTION

- Born in Canton.
- Director of religious education, St. John the Baptist Catholic Church, Canton (right).

GEORGE S. HACKETT

"Truth will prevail, and I believe that the main facts in this presentation will endure 'as long as man walks on two feet.' "
— HACKETT, IN PREFACE OF SECOND EDITION OF HIS BOOK

ABOUT

- Graduated from Cornell Medical School in 1916.
- Became an insurance examiner for 70 insurance companies, responsible for assessing the disability and recovery potential of patients. Became one of the nation's authorities on trauma and disability.
- Coined the term prolotherapy to describe a treatment that uses an injection to stimulate the growth of new ligament and tendon tissue.
- Treated more than 10,000 patients using the prolotherapy technique, and 80 percent of them reported having no pain after treatment.
- Wrote the book "Ligament and Tendon Relaxation Treatment by Prolotherapy," which still is used today by physicians learning the technique of prolotherapy.
- Mentored Dr. Gustav A. Hemwall of Illinois, who went on to master the technique, expand its use and trained many of the prolotherapy physicians who use it today.
- Died at age 81 in 1969.

STARK CONNECTION

- Began his career as a trauma surgeon at Mercy Hospital in Canton.

DR. CHARLES A. BELISLE

"We have lost more than a fine young doctor,"

—DR. WALTER H. KASSERMAN, HEART SPECIALIST WHO PIONEERED THE USE OF THE PACEMAKER IN CANTON, REPOSITORY ARTICLE FROM DEC. 7, 1966.

ABOUT

- Born: 1927 in Baton Rouge, La.
- Died: 1966 in Canton.
- Surgeon and heart specialist.

STARK CONNECTION

- Died less than a week after successfully using the first "artificial kidney" in Canton at Aultman Hospital.
- Was working to start an emphysema clinic for Canton's Goodwill Industries when he died.

150

L.B. HARTUNG

A house built in 1908 by Hartung and his wife, the former Wilhelmina "Minnie" Balser, was donated to the Philamatheon Society for the Blind during the 1950s. In 2002, the house was moved from Tuscarawas Avenue W around the corner to Wertz Avenue NW.

ABOUT

- Born in Kempton, Bavaria, in Germany in 1851 and came to the United States in 1871. Settling in Canton three years later, he used his skills as a machinist to get a job with C. Aultman Co.
- Began working in 1884 as a plumbing and boiler contractor. He patented and manufactured the home comfort boiler system. Hartung sold his business to Mahoning Valley Supply Co. in 1908.
- Invested in Belden Brick Co., eventually holding a 30 percent interest. Served on the board for more than 10 years, before becoming the company's president in 1920 following the death of Henry S. Belden. Served as company president until 1935.

STARK CONNECTION

- Lived in Canton from 1874 until is death in 1935.

DALE C. HALL

"My sincere thanks go out to all of you whom I have inconvenienced by my embarkation upon unknown and uncharted seas. Godspeed to all of you on your own individual journeys, and may they too be replete with joy and happiness."

— WRITTEN BY DALE C. HALL FOR HIS FUNERAL SERVICE.

ABOUT

- An original member of Canton's Tax Commission when the city instituted an income tax in 1952.
- Assigned by then-Mayor Thomas H. Nichols in May 1950 to "survey the books" of the Canton City Lines, a bus company that served the city. Hall's work helped the city and bus company reach a compromise fare of three tokens for 25 cents, keeping prices low and assuring enough revenue for the company.

STARK CONNECTION

- Formed Hall, Kistler & Co. certified public accounting firm in 1941 with C. Rex Kistler. Managed the firm until his death at age 70 in March 1964. Both had worked in the Canton office of Ernst & Ernst, a Cleveland-based accounting firm. Hall had managed Ernst & Ernst offices in Erie, Pa., and Canton before being named a partner, but he gave up the partnership to form a firm in Canton.
- In March 1942, named the Canton chairman for the Ohio Defense Savings Staff, which sold bonds to help fund World War II efforts.

HARRY SCHMUCK

"I have no quarrel with these guys who play golf, but I'll tell you, I get my exercise out there with my cows."

ABOUT

- Born Jan. 4, 1915. Died Aug. 22, 2001.
- Earned law degree from Cornell and practiced law nearly 60 years.
- Was a defense attorney in the 1977 trial related to the bombing of Massillon restaurant La Cuisina, where three firefighters died when the building collapsed following the explosion.
- Served as village solicitor in East Canton for 30 years.
- Provided free legal services to the elderly and people with special needs following his 1997 retirement.
- Helped incorporate the Domestic Violence Project.

STARK CONNECTION

- Practiced law in Canton.
- Lived on a dairy farm in Osnaburg Township.

RYAN MEINERDING

"We're more or less the bridge between the comics and the real world."

ABOUT

- Born April 5, 1977, in Canton.
- Graduated in 1995 from Hoover High School. Earned a bachelor's degree in industrial design from the University of Notre Dame.
- As head of visual development for Marvel Studios, he designs and oversees a team of artists creating characters and imagery for Marvel's films.
- Has worked on multiple "Iron Man," "Avengers," Captain America" and "Thor" films, among others.

STARK CONNECTION

- Credits hometown comic books shops Comics, Cards and Collectables and Land of Cran with fueling his interest in superheroes.
- Appeared at the recent Hall of Fame City Comic Con at Canton Memorial Civic Center.

RANDALL CRAIG FLEISCHER

"If you love music, there's a high likelihood you will love symphonic music. It's pure emotion in sound. It's the original unplugged."

ABOUT

- Born March 14, 1958, in Canton.
- In his seventh year as music director of the Youngstown Symphony Orchestra, and also is music director of the Anchorage (Alaska) Symphony Orchestra and Hudson Valley Philharmonic in Poughkeepsie, N.Y.
- Received critical praise in the New York Times in 1995 for conducting the New York City Opera production of Mozart's "The Magic Flute." In 1993, conducted a private concert for Pope John Paul II at the Vatican in Rome.

- Co-created and arranged the classical rock-opera fusion concert titled "Rocktopia: Live in Budapest" airing on PBS and going on a U.S. tour in Spring 2017.
- Composed "Echoes," a six-movement symphonic salute to the indigenous peoples of Alaska, Hawaii and New England that was performed at the Smithsonian Institution in Washington, D.C.

STARK CONNECTION

- Graduated from McKinley High School.

CHARLES DOUGHERTY

"I bid you welcome to this, the best city on the American continent."

— DOUGHERTY, SPEAKING ABOUT CANTON

ABOUT

- Born Oct. 28, 1850. Died Jan. 23, 1944.
- Served as president of Canton's Board of Trade, which was organized in 1885 to bring new industry to the city.
- Traveled around the country using his own money to meet with business leaders to try to persuade them to move to Canton.
- Got Henry Timken, John Carnahan and

John Dueber to relocate to the city.
- Launched a campaign in 1906 to raise $20,000 to purchase three manufacturing plants to donate to new businesses.

STARK CONNECTION

- Was born in Greentown. Died in Canton.
- Credited with building Canton's industrial base.

153

LINDA MOTTICE CLEMENS

"It all started on a Saturday afternoon, when my mother took me and my two older brothers to Canton Skateland ... and told them to watch after me. Well, they put skates on me and I never saw them the rest of the afternoon. It was either sink or swim!"

ABOUT

- Born July 5, 1944, in Canton. Lives in Sarasota, Fla.
- Performed and coached in roller skating.
- With partner Adolph Wacker was seven-time Senior Dance champion, and two-time World Champion. ▪ Also was a two-time Senior Ladies Figure champion.
- After her skating career, she became a coach, guiding many national and world champions.
- Served as coach of artistic roller sports for Pan Am Games in Winnipeg and Rio de Janeiro.
- Named coach of the year for artistic roller sports for 2000 by the U.S. Olympic Committee.
- Inducted into Skater Hall of Fame and Coaches Hall of Fame for United States Amateur Roller Skating Association.

STARK CONNECTION

- 1962 graduate of Lincoln High School.
- Began skating at Canton Skateland at age 10.

R. KIRKLAND GABLE

"His comments about education captured his ideal for thinking in general: that we should always aim toward a bolder comprehension of what the world and we ourselves, and the people around us, might become."

— ERIC SCHWITZGEBEL, ON HIS FATHER

ABOUT

- Born March 21, 1934, in Canton. Died Jan. 18, 2015.
- Along with his twin brother, Robert, invented the location-monitoring system for offenders used in ankle bracelets.
- Also served as an attorney, and wrote on the intersection of law and psychology. One of his articles was cited in a majority opinion of the Supreme Court of the United States.
- Served as a professor of psychology at Cal Lutheran University from 1975-2004.
- He and his brother changed their name from Schwitzgebel when they began publishing academic journals.

STARK CONNECTION

- 1952 graduate of North Canton High School, and also attended Lehman High School in Canton. He attended Heidelberg College, and received his bachelor's from Ohio State University and a master's in education and two doctorates from Harvard, one in counseling psychology and the other a juris doctorate.
- He also received a doctorate in social psychology from City University Los Angeles.

WILLIAM DABERKO

"Just as Daberko's career as a merchandiser was forged from hard work, devotion to duty and a desire to learn, so, too, his ability as an after-dinner speaker was developed largely through his own efforts and without the benefit of special instruction. Aided by an active imagination and a refreshing sense of humor, it 'just came naturally.' "

— THE CANTON REPOSITORY, AUG. 28, 1955.

ABOUT

- Born Aug. 29, 1880. Died Feb. 1, 1965.
- Former director of the Canton Chamber of Commerce.
- Former director of Canton Retail Merchants Board.
- Former vice president and secretary of The C.N. Vicary Co.

STARK CONNECTION

- Great-grandfather of Canton Municipal Judge Curt Werren
- Served for many years as Sunday school superintendent and Sunday school teacher at First Reformed Church.
- Was an avid bowler, forming a team with family members.

PATRICK REBILLOT

"From his start as a 12-year-old organist at St. Louis Church in Louisville, he moved to New York City and became a renowned and well-respected musician from the 1960s into 2000, performing with an all-star array of instrumentalists and singers. He was awarded the National Academy of Recording Arts and Sciences Most Valuable Keyboardist for Studio Musicians MVP recognition. In addition, he did countless TV and radio commercials and movie scores along with recording his own compositions."

— JANE MATHIE OF LOUISVILLE, REBILLOT'S SISTER

ABOUT

- Born April 21, 1935, in Louisville. Lives in New York.
- Graduated from Cincinnati College Conservatory of Music.
- Is a U.S.-based keyboard session and studio musician.
- He is associated with fellow session and studio musicians Hugh McCracken, Tony Levin, Steve Gadd, Ray Barretto and Ralph MacDonald. He also appears on recordings by John Klemmer, Steely Dan, Average White Band, Gloria Gaynor, Irene Worth, Bette Midler, Flora Purim, Hall & Oates and David Newman, among others.
- Cut his own record, "Free Fall."

STARK CONNECTION

- Was the youngest organist at St. Louis Catholic Church when he was 12.
- Graduated from Louisville High School.

ASHLEY SPENCER

"Follow your heart and pursue your dreams because anything is possible."

ABOUT

- Born March 8, 1985, in Canton.
- Appeared on Broadway in "Grease" (as Sandy), "Hairspray" (as Amber Von Tussle), "Rock of Ages" (as Sherrie) and "Priscilla, Queen of the Desert" (as a Diva).
- Placed second in the 2007 NBC reality series "Grease: You're the One That I Want," designed to cast the leads in a Broadway revival of "Grease."
- Was the understudy for Barbie in the national tour of "Barbie in Fairytopia."
- Appearing through Oct. 23 in "The Producers" (as Ulla) at Paper Mill Playhouse, Millburn, N.J.
- Is married to actor-singer Jeremy Jordan, a Tony Award nominee for "Newsies."

STARK CONNECTION

- Graduated from Jackson High School in 2003.
- Appeared locally in Players Guild productions of "A Christmas Carol," "Cinderella," "Rocky Horror Show" and "Children of Eden."

PERCY SNOW

"Offenses simply dreaded playing against him because he didn't just make the tackle; he damaged people. Percy was the hardest-hitting kid that played at Michigan State in many, many years."

— FORMER MSU COACH GEORGE PERLES

ABOUT

- Born Nov. 5, 1967, in Canton.
- Two-time first-team All-American linebacker at Michigan State, where he was a three-year starter and led the Spartans in tackles from 1987-89.
- Became the first player to win both the Lombardi Award (given to the best lineman or linebacker in college football) and the Butkus Award (given to the top linebacker) in the same year (1989).
- Drafted in the first round (13th overall) by the Kansas City Chiefs in 1990 and was named to that season's All-Rookie Team, but suffered a season-ending knee injury in a scooter accident in training camp in 1991 and never fully recovered.
- Named to the College Football Hall of Fame in 2013.
- His younger brother, Eric, played as a guard in the NBA for the SuperSonics, 76ers and Cavaliers from 1995-2009.

STARK CONNECTION

- Was a standout linebacker at McKinley High School, where he scored 137 career points and earned first team All-Ohio as a senior in 1985.

DARYL REVOLDT

ABOUT

- Born March 27, 1951, in Lansing, Mich.
- Graduated with a bachelor's and master's degrees in history from Miami University in 1973 and 1975. Earned a Ph.D in history from University of Akron in 1981.
- Regional economic representatives for the Ohio Department of Development from 2001-06.
- Director of government affairs for Techni-Graphics in Wooster from 2006-11.
- Worked as a legislative affairs and outreach director for JobsOhio from 2007-11.

STARK CONNECTION

- Grew up in Perry Township but has lived in North Canton since age 13.
- Former executive director of the Stark County Republican Party.
- Worked for then-U.S. Rep. Ralph Regula from 1985-2001, starting as an administrative aide and eventually become a district director.
- North Canton Ward 4 councilman from 1981-98 when as council president he became North Canton's mayor on Mayor Bill Hines' resignation.
- Elected to hold the seat in 1999 and was mayor until 2001 when he resigned. At-large councilman and council president from 2007 to 2011.
- Played key role in planning and approving North Canton's Main Street widening and

> "This is a wonderful opportunity to have a role in improving Ohio's employment picture."
> — REVOLDT, UPON TAKING OHIO DEPARTMENT OF DEVELOPMENT JOB

construction of new streetscape with lights and brick motif in the 1990s. He also helped oversee expanding and rebuilding of the city's water system, storm sewer system and reconstruction of roads with curbs and gutters.
- Campaigned for annexation of Washington Square into North Canton.
- Executive director of workforce and economic development for Stark State College.

CAPT. WILLIAM S. WILLIAMS

"W.S. Williams, Capt. 3d O[hio] Battery & Chief of Artillery, 3d Div[ision], 17th Army Corps Army of the Tenn[essee]"

—TOMB INSCRIPTION PENNED BY WILLIAMS A FEW DAYS BEFORE HIS DEATH IN 1923.

ABOUT

- Born: April 23, 1836, in Canton.
- Died: Feb. 16, 1923, in Canton.
- Fought at Shiloh, Vicksburg, Kennesaw Mountain and other Civil War battles and was wounded in the eye.
- Commanded Union artillery during the siege of Atlanta.
- Worked at Library of Congress, 1907 to 1910.

STARK CONNECTION

- Served as county surveyor, city engineer and state railway inspector.
- Pioneer of local brick industry.
- One of the last Civil War vets in Canton who could recall meeting Gen. Ulysses S. Grant.
- Lived at Pine Hill, his estate at the northwest corner of Cleveland Avenue and 12th Street NW.

JIM MUZZY

"Jim Muzzy built the reputation that WHBC has for sports coverage. I'm just trying to carry that on."

— JIM JOHNSON, WHO SUCCEEDED MUZZY AS WHBC'S SPORTS DIRECTOR

ABOUT

- Longtime sports director at WHBC.
- Broadcast nearly 4,000 sporting events — from baseball to racing to a national marbles tournament.
- President of the Ohio Sportscasters Association.

STARK CONNECTION

- Died at age 75 on Sept. 12, 1989, in Canton.
- Dubbed "the voice of Stark County sports."
- Served for 25 years as master of ceremonies at Pro Football Hall of Fame inductions.

RANSOM BARR

"The board expects you to carry out these instructions to the letter," Barr wrote on behalf of the school board, in a letter to the superintendent in 1950, telling him to make sure all 361 Middlebranch High students returned to school. All but 19 students had imposed a strike to support a teacher who was having difficulty with the board.

ABOUT

- Born April 11, 1898. Died Aug. 16, 1971.
- Arrested as a juvenile in 1916 for running his "machine" (car) too close to a streetcar.

STARK CONNECTION

- A 26-year member of Plain Local Schools Board of Education.
- Active in Rotary and his church.
- Director of local, state and national dairy associations.
- Barr Elementary School in Plain Township named for him.
- His family farm on 39th Street NE was converted to Meadowlake Golf Course.
- Operated a dairy and apple orchard on his farm near Martindale Road NE.
- President of Stark County Christian Endeavor.

ROBERT PINN

Pinn displayed "more than ordinary ability in the examination of witnesses and the trial of causes. He was a fluent and forceful speaker without bombast or flourish."

— TRIBUTE BY THE STARK COUNTY BAR ASSOCIATION AT THE TIME OF PINN'S DEATH.

ABOUT

- Born March 1, 1843, in Perry Township. Died Jan. 1, 1911, in Massillon.
- Enlisted in Company I, 5th United States Colored Troops Infantry/127th Ohio Volunteer Infantry in 1863.
- Fought in Virginia in New Market Heights and Petersburg; wounded three times.
- Awarded the Medal of Honor on April 6, 1865, for bravery during the Battle of New Market Heights.
- Attended Oberlin College; admitted to the Ohio Bar Association; taught school in Cairo, Ill., and Newberry, S.C.; claim agent, U.S. Prison Bureau; Teamster and contractor Mason; member of Hart Post 134, Grand Army of the Republic.
- Delegate, Ohio Republican Convention, which nominated William McKinley for governor.

KARL KING

"I've sung my song. It was a rather simple one; it wasn't too involved. I'm happy about it."

— KING, IN 1966, WHEN HE DECIDED TO STOP DIRECTING

ABOUT

- Born Feb. 21, 1891 in Paintersville, Ohio.
- Died March 31, 1971, in Fort Dodge, Iowa.
- Wrote "Barnum & Bailey's Favorite" in 1913, the Barnum & Bailey Circus theme song.
- Became bandmaster with the circus' "Greatest Show on Earth."
- Composed more than 200 marches and 100 waltzes and serenades.

STARK CONNECTION

- Family moved to Canton when he was 11 years old.
- Sold newspapers for money to buy a cornet in Canton; exchanged it for a euphonium to play in the Canton Marine Band.
- Quit school at 14 to learn the printing trade for a local newspaper, writing compositions at night.
- Directed the Grand Army Band of Canton in 1919.

M.J. ALBACETE

"One of my ambitions was to move the museum from being somewhat of a hometown museum to the point where it was offering exhibits that had a wider draw. Our goal was to bring a lot more people from other parts of Ohio and the country."

ABOUT

- Born July 23, 1939, in Canton.
- Graduated from McKinley High School; bachelor of arts in English from Walsh University; master's degree in English from the University of Akron.

STARK CONNECTION

- Executive director of the Canton Museum of Art, 1988 to 2014; associate director of the museum, 1979 to 1988.

- During Albacete's tenure, the museum's permanent collection increased in appraised value from $6 million to $25 million.
- Was instrumental in bringing the blockbuster exhibition "Kimono As Art" to the museum in 2009. Other noteworthy shows include Andrew Wyeth's "Helga" paintings, Norman Rockwell and local artist Clyde Singer.

DICK SNYDER

"When it came to athletics, Dick could do just about anything he wanted to. That even included riding a bicycle better than anybody else."

— LONGTIME COLLEGE BASKETBALL COACH "LEFTY" DRIESELL

ABOUT

- Born Feb. 1, 1944, in North Canton.
- 13-year NBA career included 11,755 points, the 17th most in NBA history at the time of his retirement in 1979.
- Averaged 19.1 points in 1970-71, the highest single-season scoring average by a Stark County native in the NBA until C.J. McCollum's 20.8 in 2015-16 with Portland.

- Won 1979 NBA championship with Seattle SuperSonics.
- Made winning shot in Game 7 of Cavaliers' Miracle of Richfield playoffs series against Washington in 1976.
- All-American and Southern Conference Player of the Year in basketball for "Lefty" Driesell at Davidson College, where he also played baseball.

160

TOMMY HENRICH

"(Henrich) got more pure joy out of baseball than any player I ever knew."

— FAMED SPORTS WRITER RED SMITH.

ABOUT

- Born Feb. 20, 1913 in Massillon.
- Died Dec. 1, 2009, in Dayton, at age 96. Was oldest living Yankee before his death and the last living teammate of Lou Gehrig.
- Won seven World Series during his 11 seasons with the New York Yankees.
- Helped the Yankees average 97.5 wins during his career from 1937-42 and 1946-50 — as he served in the Coast Guard during World War II.
- Hit the first walk-off homer in World Series history (Game 1, 1949) and tied a league record with four grand slams in 1948.
- Selected to five American League All-Star teams — leading the AL in runs in 1948 and in triples twice.
- Hit .282 for his career with 183 home runs, 795 RBIs and 901 runs.
- Hit 12 game-winning home runs in the first 65 games of the 1949 season, when he hit cleanup in place of the injured Joe DiMaggio.

STARK CONNECTION

- Graduated from St. John's Catholic High School in Canton.
- Caught the attention of Major League scouts in the early 1930s playing for semipro teams while also working as a typist at Republic Steel.

DAVID HIBBARD

"I'm a huge fan of Canton. I go back every second I can. There are seven girls and three boys in my family. My sister lives across the street from my mom, there are cousins next door and across the street — and it's a dead-end street. As you can imagine, it's a commune."

ABOUT

- Born June 21, 1965 in Spokane, Wash.
- Actor in Broadway shows and musicals.
- Has performed in such shows as "Cats," "Monty Python's Spamalot," and "Billy Elliot The Musical."
- Graduate of Ohio State University with a degree in music education and on faculty at CAP21, a New York City professional musical theatre training conservatory and Off-Broadway Theatre company.
- Performed in outdoor shows at Kings Island while in college.
- Does voiceover work in New York, and was narrator for the series "Page to Screen" on Bravo.

STARK CONNECTION

- 1983 GlenOak High School graduate.
- Performed in theater productions while at GlenOak.

161

CHARLES R. FRAZER

"During the 33 years (as superintendent of the Canton Humane Society), Frazer has found homes for several hundred children, many of them babies."

— THE EVENING REPOSITORY, MARCH 11, 1916

ABOUT

- Born Sept. 8, 1858, in Canton.
- Died Nov. 27, 1916, in Canton.
- Newspaperman, politician, activist.

STARK CONNECTION

- Worked for The Evening Repository and News-Democrat.

- Member of Canton City Council and Board of Trade.
- Looked after the welfare of animals and found homes for orphans and abandoned children as superintendent of the Canton Humane Society.

ASHLEY (MUFFET) DUNCAN

ABOUT

- Competed in the U.S. Olympic Trials for shot put in 2008 and 2012.
- Four-time All-American at the University of Kentucky from 2006-10 and holds Kentucky's school records in the shot put and discus.
- Assistant track and field coach at Ohio State University. Previously spent two seasons as assistant throws coach at Western Kentucky, where she was instrumental in the development of the school's first female qualifier for the NCAA outdoor championships in three individual events.
- 2014 U.S. Track and Field and Cross Country Coaches Association Southeast Region Women's Assistant Coach of the Year.

"Ashley has been a tremendous athlete for us, and no one has had as much interest and passion as she has. She has been very successful and has had some disappointments, but at this high level, those can be very close. Ashley's contributions in three different events have been very valuable and will be almost impossible to replace."

— DON WEBER, HEAD TRACK COACH AT THE UNIVERSITY OF KENTUCKY, IN JUNE 2010 WHEN MUFFET ENDED HER COLLEGE CAREER.

STARK CONNECTION

- 2005 Hoover High School graduate.
- One of only two female athletes in Stark County history with three individual track and field state championships.
- Won back-to-back Division I state titles in the shot put in 2004 and 2005, setting a state record as a high school senior.
- Won a state championship in the discus in 2005. Her marks of 50 feet, 10 inches in the shot put and 162-4 in the discus remain all-time county records.
- Goalkeeper for the Hoover Vikings soccer team.

SAMUEL W. SPECK JR.

"Sam Speck has contributed in countless ways to the quality and vitality of life in Ohio and the Great Lakes region as a farsighted public administrator, legislator, conservationist, and educator."

— OHIO GOV. BOB TAFT IN HIS NOMINATION OF SPECK FOR THE NATIONAL GOVERNORS ASSOCIATION AWARD.

ABOUT

- Served in the Ohio General Assembly as both a state representative and state senator (R- New Concord) for 13 years starting in 1971.
- Associate director of the Federal Emergency Management Agency under President Ronald Reagan.
- Ohio's Director of Natural Resources for eight years; served on the Ohio Lake Erie Commission and the Great Lakes Commission.
- Appointed by President George W. Bush to the International Joint Commission in 2008.
- A graduate of Muskingum University and president of the university from 1988 to 1999.
- In 2004, received the National Governors Association's annual award for Distinguished Service in State Government.
- Earned a master's degree at Harvard University. Studied abroad in Africa, including a 16-month trip with his wife, Sharon.

STARK CONNECTION

- A native of Nimishillen Township, born Jan. 31, 1937.
- A 1955 graduate of Louisville High School.

STANLEY CMICH

"Those who can remember him know he was a great man. He really, really always had the best interests of the city of Canton at heart."

— REPOSITORY STORY

ABOUT

- Born Aug. 13, 1916, Glen Campbell, Pa. Died Jan. 24, 2009.
- World War II veteran, earned two Purple Hearts with the First Armored Division.
- Worked as Cuyahoga County sheriff's deputy, then Ohio Department of Liquor Control enforcement chief of the Akron district and Canton liquor control agent in 1950, racking up 101 citations and making 90 arrests in one year.

STARK CONNECTION

- Canton Safety Director, 1951 to 1957
- Canton Junior Chamber of Commerce Outstanding Young Man of 1953; Ohio Jaycees Distinguished Service Award.
- Longest serving mayor in Canton history, from 1964 to 1983; oversaw construction of a new wastewater treatment plant, New-Market downtown development, renovation of the Memorial Civic Center; broke ground for the Southeast Community Center.

JENNA LILLEY

"She worked harder than anyone that I ever coached."

— HOOVER HEAD COACH JERRY GOODPASTURE

ABOUT
- Born July 2, 1996, in North Canton.
- Three-time first-team All-Ohioan and four-time All-Ohioan in softball for Hoover High School, which was the first Division I school to go 34-0 in winning the 2013 state softball championship.
- Batted .690 and was named Ohio's Gatorade Player of the Year in 2013.
- Ranked the No. 1 high school recruit by StudentSports.com her senior year, when she became the first Ohio player to receive a Division I scholarship from the Pac-12 when she signed with Oregon.
- Made second team NFCA All-American as a true freshman for Oregon in 2015, when she led the Ducks in batting average at .427 and scored 60 runs and drove in 44.

Started for USA Softball's Junior Women's National Team that won the gold medal in 2015 and earned a spot on the 2016 USA Softball's Women's National Team.

STARK CONNECTION
- Starred on four Hoover Vikings teams that won state championships in 2011-14, a feat duplicated just once in Ohio softball.

JOSEPH N. SMITH

ABOUT
- Born April 15, 1930, in Demopolis, Ala. Died June 1, 2000.
- Graduate, McKinley High School; North Carolina A&T State University; and advanced studies, Kent State University.
- Service includes: Aultman Hospital board chairman; vice president, Central Regional Council of the National Urban League Executive Directors; president, Ohio Urban League Executive Directors; Selective Service Commission; Canton Junior Chamber of Commerce; planning commission, United Negro College Fund Drive; life member, Stark County NAACP; Canton Rotary Club; Canton Negro Oldtimers Association; Canton City Schools Business Advisory Committee; Pro Football Hall of Fame Festival Grand Parade Committee; Private Industry Council of Wayne & Stark Counties; Canton-Stark-Wayne CETA Consortium Advisory Council; Omega Psi Phi Fraternity; Canton Frontiers Social Club; chairman, Stark County Grand Jury.
- Group worker, Boys Village Treatment Center.
- Participant, 1963 March on Washington.

STARK CONNECTION
- Lifelong Canton resident.
- Executive director, Canton Urban League for 38 years.

"He lived his dream. He believed in this community. He believed in the inclusiveness of this community, he really did."

— REPOSITORY STORY

BEA McPHERSON

"They wouldn't tell us what day. We knew it was going to be something big, but we didn't know it would be that big."

— McPHERSON TALKING ABOUT WORKING ON THE NORMANDY MAPS TO THE CANTON REPOSITORY IN 1984.

ABOUT
- Born 1921.
- Military Mapping Maiden during World War II.
- Prepared maps for American troops, including for the invasion of Normandy and the Battle of the Bulge.
- Inducted into the Geospatial Intelligence Hall of Fame on Oct. 4.

STARK CONNECTION
- Born in Canton.
- Recruited in 1942 from Kent State University by the Army Map Service.
- Settled in the Hartville area after the war.

LARRY PULKA

"The first wooden boat model kit I tried, it was like I'd done this before."

ABOUT
- Runs Blue Water Majesty Museum, where he displays his model ships.
- Uses exotic wood with natural color rather than paint or stain.
- Used parts of 240 beef bones to build the Confederacy, which was valued at nearly $54,000.
- Built the Frigate of 1778 from 158,326 pieces from 42 kinds of wood.
- Has had visitors at the museum from Europe, Asia and South America.

STARK CONNECTION
- Opened his museum in 2007.
- Has shown his work at the Cultural Center and the Canton Museum of Art.

DACIAN O. BARRETTE

"Two lonely buildings in the midst of large alfalfa fields and bare lawns, which Brother Dacian Barrette strong-armed Student-Brothers to adorn with trees."

— ROBERT ALFRED SMYTH, CLASS OF 1964, SHARED HIS FIRST IMPRESSION OF THE SCHOOL IN THE FALL 2014 WALSH TIMES NEWSLETTER.

ABOUT

- Born Jan. 5, 1916, in Fall River, Mass. Died Oct. 4, 1997, in Canton.
- Held degrees from Montreal University, St. Michael's College and Notre Dame.
- Came to Canton area in 1960.

STARK CONNECTION

- One of the seven Brothers of Christian Instruction who founded Walsh College (now Walsh University), turning an alfalfa field into a college campus.

Served as school's business officer until leaving in 1973 to study for the priesthood.
- Priest at St. Anthony in Canton, from 1979-1986 and 1994-1995.
- Also served at St. Barbara in Massillon and St. Paul in Canton.
- Honored as a monsignor in 1997, while at St. Therese in Brewster.
- The Business and Community Center at Walsh is named for him.
- A business major alumni scholarship at Walsh is named for him.

KIMBERLE WILLIAMS CRENSHAW

"Any denial of citizenship seems to be a way around the basic guarantees of citizenship, including rights against unlawful treatment, torture, and cruel and unusual punishment ... the Constitution should not be so easily circumvented."

ABOUT

- Born in 1959 in Canton.
- Professor of law at UCLA and Columbia University; expert on constitutional law, feminism and gender issues; credited with coining the terms "critical race theory" and "intersectionality."
- Graduate, McKinley High School; Cornell University; University of Wisconsin School of Law; Harvard Law School.
- Served on the legal team for Anita Hill during the Supreme Court confirmation hearings for

Justice Clarence Thomas.
- Executive director of the African American Policy Forum; founder, Center for Intersectionality & Social Policy Studies.
- Fulbright Scholar for Latin America (Brazil).
- Credited with influencing South Africa to insert an "equality" clause in its constitution.
- Named to Ebony Magazine's "Power 100."

STARK CONNECTION

- Daughter of the late Walter and Marian Crenshaw, Canton City Schools educators.

HERBERT T.O. BLUE

"The man with the unforgettable name and the almost unforgettable mind is gone. … His wide-ranging interest in history and the energy with which he carried on (his) research inspired everybody who watched him work."

— REPOSITORY EDITORIAL ON OCT. 15, 1963, FOLLOWING BLUE'S DEATH

ABOUT

- Born Sept. 9, 1887, in Ada, Ohio. Died Oct. 13, 1963.
- Authored numerous books and articles on a variety of historical topics, such as the Indian and pioneer history of northeastern Ohio and the centennial history of Hardin County.
- Taught in the Kenton, Ada and Dunkirk school districts.
- Said in 1934 that he had clasped hands with every Ohio governor, except two, since William McKinley's tenure between 1892 and 1896.

STARK CONNECTION

- Published the book, "History of Stark County, Ohio: From the age of prehistoric man to the present day" in 1928, as well as a history of the Canton Lodge and compiled the genealogical history of numerous Canton families.
- Taught high school history and English in the Canton City School District for more than 30 years, retiring in 1954.
- Wrote the history of the Canton Lodge Free & Accepted Masons in 1946.
- Member and elder emeritus of the First Christian Church of Canton. He taught the Loyal Men's Bible Class for more than 40 years.

EDWARD "PEEL" COLEMAN

"Peel, in my mind, was able to meet the people's needs. He made people feel like he was their councilman. I thought he was a good councilman. He was a gentle giant."

— CANTON CITY COUNCILMAN THOMAS WEST, D-2.

ABOUT

- Born Oct. 15, 1922, in Albany, Ga. Died Sept. 11, 2000, in Canton.
- Served on Canton City Council from Jan. 1, 1974, until Dec. 31, 2001, representing Ward 2.
- Assisted in naming Thurman Munson Memorial Stadium in Canton.
- Advocated to increase the number of racial minorities on the Canton Fire and Police departments.

STARK CONNECTION

- The Edward "Peel" Coleman Center at 1400 Sherrick Road SE is named in his honor.
- Served as an umpire in youth baseball programs in Canton.
- Retired from the former Ford Motor Co. plant.

TOM SCHERVISH

"I said this in 1975 when I received the coveted Distinguished Service Award from the Canton Jaycees: 'Stark County is a great place to live, work, and play.' There is no better place to raise a family."

ABOUT
- Bachelor's degree from University of Detroit.
- Owner and chairman of Stark Management Services.

STARK CONNECTION
- Board member, Pro Football Hall of Fame, past chairman; Brewster Dairy; co-owner of Center Ice Sports Complex; member of Rotary Club of Canton.
- Past board member Walsh University; Canton Country Day School; Central Catholic Advisory Board; Canton Tomorrow; Downtown Canton Land Bank Foundation; and Greater Canton Chamber of Commerce (current member of the Downtown Canton Partnership).

WILLIAM HENRY "BOSS" HOOVER

"The sum total of his aim in life was to lead men Godward. Over his desk was a card which said in large letters 'God First,' and that was the secret of his life. He lived a life so transparent that the light of God and heaven shone through him ..."

ABOUT
- Born Aug. 18, 1849. Died Feb. 25, 1932.
- Initially manufactured leather goods in New Berlin.
- Purchased patent for vacuum cleaner from his in-law James Murray Spangler.
- In 1908, founded what would become the Hoover Co.
- Built factories in North Canton, then in Canada in 1911 and England in 1919.
- His marketing efforts and free trials propelled Hoover Co, into largest vacuum maker in the world.

STARK CONNECTION
- High school in North Canton is named after Hoover Co.
- Helped establish library.
- First mayor of North Canton.
- Financed early housing developments in North Canton.
- The Hoover Co. ceased operations in North Canton in 2007.

WILLIAM STRASSNER

"A hale 83 years of age, Mr. Strassner is one of the original 18 members of the band, named in honor of H. Clark Thayer, a teacher who helped in its foundation."

— THE REPOSITORY STATED IN STRASSNER'S RETIREMENT ARTICLE IN 1958.

ABOUT
- Born in 1874; died in 1958.
- Directed the Thayer Military Band for 55 years, then was director emeritus and treasurer of the band after his retirement.

STARK CONNECTION
- The Canton-based military band formed in the 1800s.

- Band members played at Gov. McKinley's inauguration in Columbus and during the former president's funeral procession.
- In 1968, the military band later merged with the American Legion Band and the Nazir Grotto Band to form what's known today as the Canton Concert Band.

SHEILA FISHER

"Women have a tremendous impact in our society and too often their value has gone unrecognized. If this is going to be the only institution dedicated to the history of our first ladies in America, it should be done perfectly."

— SHEILA FISHER, VICE PRESIDENT IN CHARGE OF RESTORATION, RENOVATION & ACQUISITIONS FOR THE NATIONAL FIRST LADIES LIBRARY

ABOUT
- Born July 20, 1932, in Cornwall, Ontario, Canada.
- Married Jack Fisher; three children, six grandchildren.
- A clinical psychologist, earning her degrees at Case Western Reserve University.

STARK CONNECTION
- Founder and president of the Stark County Suicide Prevention and Crisis Help Center; served as a professional consultant for 10 years.
- Vice president in charge of Restoration, Renovation & Acquisitions for the National First Ladies Library — full-time volunteer and president emeritus.

- Received Mental Health Volunteer of the Year Award from Stark County Mental Health Association.
- Listed on The Wall of Fame by the Ohio Bicentennial Committee, Who's Who in Ohio, Who's Who of American Women.
- Volunteer for Aultman Hospital Women's Board, Angel of the Canton Museum of Art, advisory board of The Schepens Eye Research in Boston, Mount Union College Advisory Board.
- Author of "Suicide and Crisis Prevention: A Guide to Services," in use at universities and crisis centers.
- Award of Merit from the Ohio Historical Society, Ohio History Preservation Office Award of Outstanding contributions to historic preservation in Ohio.

DOROTHY PATTERSON SAYRE

"If you look closely at the marvelous tapestry of living, you will see that the shining thread of caring runs through it all like a streak of golden fire."

ABOUT

- Was one of Canton's youngest female lawyers and was the first woman elected to serve on the Stark County Bar Association executive committee.
- Developed a naturalization program for new citizens that earned national recognition and included each new citizen receiving a letter from the president.
- Chaired the American citizenship committee of the Stark County Bar Association and was responsible for 2,500 new citizens in Stark County from 70 countries.

- Served as president of the nonprofit organization Quota International from 1963 to 1965.
- Was an adjutant and lieutenant in the Civil Air Patrol.
- Received her private pilot's license.

STARK CONNECTION

- Was a lifelong Canton resident.
- Graduated from McKinley High School, Mount Union College, William McKinley School of Law.

VERA L. ELLIOTT

"She lived for politics. She very much believed in the Democratic Party and the democratic process."

— JOAN ELLIOTT GRAY OF MADISON, WIS., VERA ELLIOTT'S DAUGHTER.

ABOUT

- Born 1910 in Wayne County; died in Stark County Nov. 2, 1987.
- Elected to Canton City Council, serving two terms, from 1946 to 1949.
- Served on Stark County Board of Elections 24 years, including time as director, keeping office open extra hours to register voters.
- President of Ohio Democratic Central Committee.
- Served as officer in Democratic Woman's

Club at both city and state levels.
- Active in the League of Women Voters and Board of Realtors.
- President of local PTA; Sunday school teacher.
- Campaigned in Ward 2 of Canton with red, white and blue streamers on her children's baby buggies.
- First Woman of the Year of the Democratic Woman's Club of Canton in 1968.
- Retired at age 71 in 1981, then died just hours before Election Day in 1987.

GRETCHEN GROETZINGER PUTNAM

"She was The Repository's 'newspaper gal'—its oldest pro on the distaff side. But we never forgot that our 'Groetz' once had been Canton's beauteous Miss Groetzinger and then had become Mrs. George F. Putnam, who was known by everybody. She was ours, but she belonged to Canton."

— REPOSITORY EDITOR ON HER DEATH

ABOUT

- Born 1888. Died June 27, 1961, at age 73.
- A beloved Repository reporter and writer for 50 years, from 1911 until shortly before her death.
- Joined the Repository as a society writer, moved to the news beat in 1919 and became a church and obituary reporter in the 1940s.
- In 1919, became one of the first women to fly in an airplane during a 50-minute flight in an open-air cockpit.
- Helped research the 1960 Pulitzer Prize-winning "In The Days of McKinley" by historian Margaret Leech.
- During World War I and II, led volunteer efforts to raise funds and knit clothing for American troops. Also joined the Red Cross Motor Corps in World War II.
- As a child, family friends with future President William McKinley.
- Married husband George F. Putnam in 1924.

STARK CONNECTION

- Lifelong Canton resident.
- 1906 graduate of Central High School.

THOMAS J. SEAMAN

"I love to fly. This is a good way to share that with other people."

— THOMAS J. SEAMAN IN 1999, ON HIS ROLE FLYING ILL PEOPLE TO GET SPECIALIZED MEDICAL CARE AT HOSPITALS AROUND THE COUNTRY.

ABOUT

- Born June 15, 1930, in Canton. Died Aug. 13, 2014, in Canton.
- Named Most Valuable Player on football team at St. Aquinas Prep School in Rochester, N.Y., in 1949.
- Played right guard for the University of Notre Dame football team from 1950-52 under Coach Frank Leahy. Graduated from Notre Dame in 1953. Earned All-American Honorable Mention.
- Pilot for 42 years and co-owner of the Pittsburgh-based Volunteer Pilots Association, whose more than 200 volunteer pilots took part in Angel Plane, in which he and other volunteer pilots provided medical transportation at their own expense for people with serious medical conditions, including transplant patients who found it difficult to travel on commercial aircraft for specialized treatments at hospitals around the country. Owned a twin-engine Beach Baron.
- A financial planner, insurance agent and adviser. Founded Seaman Retirement Planning in 1957.

STARK CONNECTION

- Grew up in Canton and was named All-Ohio as a football player for Lincoln High School, where he graduated in 1948.
- A longtime resident of Jackson Township.
- President of the Hall of Fame Luncheon Club and member for more than 30 years.
- For four years in the 1960s, was the Democratic councilman representing Canton's Ward 1.

GEORGE DEUBLE SR.

Credited with making Canton's first town clock, using parts that were forged and cast by local trade businesses. The finished clock "hung in the old court house, where it did service for many years," according to an article in Feb. 22, 1908 edition of The Evening Repository.

ABOUT

- The pioneer jeweler of Canton. He visited the area in 1831 to sell clocks and watches to settlers.
- Brought his family to Canton in 1833 by covered wagon and opened a jewelry and clock business.
- Died in 1860, leaving the business to his sons, Martin and George. Deuble's descendants operated the business for more than 100 years.

STARK CONNECTION

- The Deuble Foundation, created by the family, continues to help fund programs, projects and organizations in the community.

Oldest Canton Store, Still In Same Family, Will Be 100 Years Old April 1

EURETTA KINGSBURY BEITER

A charter member — but not among the 14 founders — of the Canton Woman's Club. In 1920, she bought shares of stock in the club to help finance its formation. She later served as club president. "Her leadership and involvement affected and influenced many lives," according to Stark County Wall of Fame.

ABOUT

- Born in Huron County in May 1883; graduated Oberlin College, and trained at Lakeside Hospital in Cleveland to become a registered nurse.
- Married Dr. J. Ross Beiter in September 1911. Both were from Huron County, and both had worked at Lakeside Hospital.
- Continued to live in Canton following her husband's death in 1936. Died Sept. 1, 1958, in Sandusky while visiting her daughter and grandchildren.

STARK CONNECTION

- Was a member of Sorosis and the Sorosis Garden Club. Sorosis was a national professional woman's group that worked to further education and social activities for women.
- Called an "untiring worker" for different committees at First Presbyterian Church.
- Active with the local chapter of the Daughters of the American Revolution and other organizations tied to the country's founding.

172

AUGUST LOEHLE

"I had heard my father tell about his trip to America and I wanted to go to the United States and get a job."

ABOUT
- Born Feb. 27, 1877, in Ueberlingen, Germany.
- Died Saturday, July 8, 1961, in Canton.
- Became an American citizen in 1910.
- Worked as an artist and interior decorator.

STARK CONNECTION
- Came to America in 1903, moved to Canton in 1908.
- Worked for the King Cole Co. in Canton then later for the Spuhler in Massillon

before starting his own business.
- He was instrumental in founding the local Swiss Country Club in 1927; decorated the club's downstairs walls with scenes from the Switzerland he remembered from when he lived there.
- Worked with the decorating company that decorated the Canton Palace Theatre. He drew the crests above the stage and on the walls.
- Member of the Swiss Singing Society of Canton and the Moose Lodge.

DANIEL WORLEY

ABOUT
- Born Feb. 28, 1829, in Harrisburg. Died in May 1888.
- Became an ordained Lutheran minister before becoming a professor in math and natural science at Capital University in Columbus for 11 years.
- Served one year as principal of a high school in Columbus and in 1863 took charge of an academy in Greensburg, Pa.
- Elected in 1877 as state representative and served one term.

STARK CONNECTION
- Served as superintendent of Canton public schools from 1865 to 1876.
- Namesake of the Canton City school building

at 1340 23rd St. NW. The original school was built in 1918 with 20 rooms and a playground on the roof that was never used.
- Started a private academy on North Poplar Street after retiring from Canton public schools.
- Ran the Democratic Press, a weekly paper in Canton, until it became a financial failure.
- Served in multiple public offices, including justice of the peace, city council and council president, county deputy auditor, school board member and member of the water works board.
- Has an 1889 Ahrens horse-drawn fire engine named after him due to his part in forming the city water works. The engine was last used in 1916 and is on display in the First Station in the Street of Shops of the McKinley Presidential Library & Museum.

"Our hope and prayer is that the incoming legislature of Ohio will not be longer deaf to the appeals which have gone up to Columbus from earnest teachers and other friends of education, now these many, many years."

— DENNIS WORLEY IN THE ANNUAL REPORT OF THE STATE COMMISSIONER OF COMMON SCHOOLS FOR THE SCHOOL YEAR ENDING AUG. 31, 1875.

CHRIS SPIELMAN

"The aura in Massillon on Friday nights was unique. On my first Friday in ninth grade there, I was the only kid in the school that didn't have on a Massillon shirt. Not just the only kid — the only person. I was like, 'Somebody's got to tell me the rules over here.'"

ABOUT

- Born Oct. 11, 1965 in Canton.
- Became the first high school athlete to make the cover of a Wheaties box as a senior at Massillon in 1983.
- A two-time All-America linebacker at Ohio State, he won the Lombardi Award in 1987 as college football's best lineman or linebacker. He was inducted into the College Football Hall of Fame in 2009.
- Drafted in the second round of the 1988 NFL draft by Detroit, where he played from 1988-95, making four Pro Bowls. Also played for the Buffalo Bills (1996-97) before retiring in 1999 after suffering a neck injury in training camp with the expansion Cleveland Browns.
- His brother, Rick, is the general manager of the Minnesota Vikings.

STARK CONNECTION

- Graduated from Massillon High School in 1984.

TIM FOX

"I remember that first year in Pop Warner. Some mothers were campaigning to keep me from playing because they thought I was hitting people too hard. I just did it the only way I knew how. When you're not a big guy, if you didn't try to hit somebody as hard as you can, they might not go down. I kind of followed that through my career."

ABOUT

- Born Nov. 1, 1953, in Canton.
- Made The Canton Repository's all-county in football as a do-everything junior at Glenwood High before battling injuries his senior season.
- Earned four letters at Ohio State and was named All-American as a senior in 1975, helping the Buckeyes go 40-5-1 and play in four consecutive Rose Bowl games.
- Drafted in the first round by the New England Patriots in 1976, making the All-Rookie team that fall and the Pro Bowl in 1980.
- Played in 91 consecutive games over six seasons for New England, then played six more years for the San Diego Chargers and Los Angeles Rams.
- His nephews, Derek and Dustin Fox, each played in the NFL.

STARK CONNECTION

- Graduated from Glenwood High School in 1972.

DENNIS FRANKLIN

"That season was pretty cool. I remember the camaraderie, how well we got along as teammates and how easy it was for us to work together for one common goal."

— DENNIS FRANKLIN ON THE 1970 MASSILLON TIGERS

ABOUT

- Born Aug. 24, 1953 in Massillon
- Recruited by legendary University of Michigan head coach Bo Schembechler, started for Wolverines all three seasons he was eligible from 1972-1974. Was the first black starter at quarterback for Michigan.
- Compiled a 30-2-1 record as starter at Michigan, sharing the Big Ten championship all three seasons. Ran for 1,212 yards and passed for 2,285 in his career.
- Finished sixth in the 1974 Heisman Trophy voting after being named to the first team All-Big Ten team.
- Chosen in the sixth round by the Detroit Lions of the 1975 NFL Draft. Played nine games for the Lions over the 1975-76 seasons, catching six passes for 125 yards, a stellar 20.8 yards a catch.

STARK CONNECTION

- Quarterbacked Massillon to its last state championship in 1970, when Tigers went 10-0 and outscored foes 412-29.

JEFF LOGAN

"I could have gone somewhere else and played, but it wouldn't have been the same. It was never more fun than playing football at North Canton in Stark County, not even at Ohio State."

— LOGAN BEFORE HE WAS INDUCTED INTO THE STARK COUNTY HIGH SCHOOL FOOTBALL HALL OF FAME IN 2003

ABOUT

- Born in 1956.
- Tailback on four Big Ten championship teams at Ohio State from 1974-77.
- Backed up two-time Heisman Trophy winner Archie Griffin for two seasons before rushing for 1,248 yards as a junior, his first year as a starter.
- Served as the color analyst on Ohio State football radio broadcasts.

STARK CONNECTION

- Fast, powerful running back for the Hoover Vikings in the early 1970s.
- Set a Stark County single-season scoring record with 216 points, a mark that stood for 33 years before it was broken by Ohio Mr. Football Keishaun Sims of Perry in 2015.
- Led Hoover to its first 10-0 season in 1972.

EARLE BRUCE

"When I went to Massillon, I had the best interview at any place I've ever gone for the job of the football coach. They talked football, not garbage, not politics. They wanted to know what the hell I was going to do to make them undefeated."

— EARLE BRUCE DURING A SPEECH AT THE PRO FOOTBALL HALL OF FAME LUNCHEON CLUB IN 2008.

ABOUT
- Born March 8, 1931, in Cumberland, Md.
- Head football coach at Ohio State from 1979-87.
- Compiled a 81-26-1 record with four Big Ten championships and two Rose Bowl appearances in eight seasons with the Buckeyes.
- Served as head football coach at Tampa and at Iowa State prior to coming to Ohio State. Also was the head coach at Northern Iowa in 1988 and at Colorado State from 1989-92.
- Inducted into the College Football Hall of Fame in 2002.

STARK CONNECTION
- Head football coach at Massillon from 1964-65.
- Remains the only undefeated coach (20-0) in school history.
- Led the Tigers to state championships both seasons.

DUSTIN FOX

"In my opinion, he was the best athlete of all of us. There was never any pressure because he was that good."

— DEREK FOX

ABOUT
- Born Oct. 8, 1982, in Canton.
- Named first team All-Ohio as a defensive back at GlenOak in 1999 and 2000.
- Member of the Golden Eagles' 400-meter relay team that still holds the Stark County record.
- Started at cornerback for four years at Ohio State, where he helped the Buckeyes win the 2002 national championship.
- Drafted in the third round by the Minnesota Vikings in 2005 and played four years in the NFL for the Vikings, Eagles and Bills.
- Uncle Tim Fox played at Ohio State and 12 years in the NFL for the Patriots, Chargers and Rams. Brother Derek played collegiately for Penn State and for the Rams and Colts in the NFL.

STARK CONNECTION
- Graduated from GlenOak High School in 2001.

MIKE DOSS

"I always wanted to help raise the team's level of play, to raise my level of play, to be respected for that. I always wanted to be the best of the best."

ABOUT

- Born March 24, 1981, in Canton.
- Played strong safety at Ohio State from 1999-2002.
- Became just the seventh three-time All-American in program history.
- Co-captain on Ohio State's 2002 national championship team. Named Fiesta Bowl Defensive MVP after the Buckeyes beat Miami (Fla.) to clinch their first national title since 1968.
- Selected by the Indianapolis Colts in the second round of the 2003 NFL Draft. Played 57 games in the NFL with Indianapolis, Minnesota and Cincinnati.

STARK CONNECTION

- A dominant runner and hard-hitting safety on McKinley's Division I state championship teams in 1997 and 1998.
- Finished his career with a school-record 15 interceptions, including one on the first play of the 1997 championship game against Cincinnati Moeller.
- Scored four touchdowns in the 1998 title game against Cincinnati St. Xavier. Rushed for 1,454 yards his senior year.

WILLIAM PITTENGER

"It was a painfully thrilling moment. We were but 20, with an army about us, and a long difficult road before us, crowded with enemies."

— WILLIAM PITTENGER, RECALLING BOARDING THE TRAIN NAMED THE "GENERAL" WITH OTHER MEMBERS OF THE 2ND OVI IN 1862, DISGUISED AS MEMBERS OF THE CONFEDERATE ARMY, TO BEGIN A MILITARY MANEUVER CALLED ANDREW'S RAID.

ABOUT

- Born 1840 in Jefferson County; died 1904 in San Diego, Calif.
- Fought in the first Battle of Bull Run.
- Medal of Honor recipient in Civil War for valor during Andrew's Raid, a secret Union army attack also called "The Great Locomotive Chase," in 1862.
- Was captured in Georgia, exchanged as a prisoner of War in 1863, and was honorably discharged with disabilities.
- Became a farmer and an author of books, including "Daring and Suffering: A History of the Great Railroad Adventurers" (1863) and "Oratory, Sacred and Secular."

STARK CONNECTION

- Served as a minister at Massillon's First Methodist Church.

177

GEORGE SAIMES

"There wasn't a better safety before him, and I don't think there's been any since. There should've been consideration for him going into the Hall of Fame."

— FORMER BILLS TEAMMATE BOOKER EDGERSON TO THE NEW YORK TIMES AFTER SAIMES' DEATH IN 2013.

ABOUT

- Born Sept. 1, 1941, in Canton. Died March 10, 2013 in North Canton.
- One of the 22 players on the American Football League's all-time team.
- Played safety for the Buffalo Bills before the AFL-NFL merger and for the Denver Broncos after the merger.
- Leader on Bills 1964 and 1965 AFL championship teams.
- Missed playing in the first Super Bowl because the game between the AFL champion and NFL champion did not begin until 1966, when the Bills reached the AFL finals but lost to Kansas City, whose Alliance-born quarterback, Len Dawson, played in Super Bowl I.

- Most valuable player at Michigan State as a fullback and defensive back in 1961 and '62.
- Finished a long career in scouting as the director of scouting for the Houston Texans.

STARK CONNECTION

- One of the Canton area's better all-around athletes, a varsity player in multiple sports at Canton Lincoln High School.
- Settled in North Canton and maintained duties as a top scout while a residence in Stark County.
- A fixture at the Belden Village Panera, for years his coffee spot with old Canton friends.

ELEANOR G. SCHMID

"Eleanor G. Schmid ... devoted public servant who aided many citizens."

— FROM ELEANOR SCHMID'S ENTRY ON THE STARK COUNTY WALL OF FAME.

ABOUT

- Born 1890 in Pennsylvania; died 1980.
- Civic leader and community volunteer.
- President of several organizations, including Canton YWCA, Altar Guild, Children's Aid Society, Canton Needlework Guild, and Northeast Ohio Diocese of the Episcopal Church.
- Member of the DAR and Woman's Club.
- Volunteer for the American Red Cross.

- Board member for the Canton Scholarship Foundation.

STARK CONNECTION

- Secretary of Aultman Home for the Aged.
- Bible School teacher for 52 years at St. Paul's Episcopal Church.
- 1958 Canton community Woman of the Year.

THOMAS WILSON SAXTON

"His friends who knew him are well aware that considerations of a nobler character, appertaining as they did to the best good of his fellow men, were paramount in fixing his choice."

— REPOSITORY EDITORIAL PUBLISHED UPON THE DEATH OF THOMAS SAXTON IN 1884.

ABOUT

- Born Oct. 9, 1831; died Nov. 2, 1884.
- Was the eighth child of John and Margaret Saxton.
- Son of The Ohio Repository's founder, who followed his father into the printing business at age 14.
- Starting as a typesetter, Saxton grew to become a partner with his father in Saxton & Son, and upon his father's death in 1871, the newspaper's second owner.
- Served as quartermaster in the 115th Ohio Volunteer Infantry during the Civil War.
- Converted The Ohio Repository into a daily newspaper in 1878.

STARK CONNECTION

- Served as Stark County auditor.
- Married Maria Slanker of Canton on March 30, 1857, on the anniversary of the date his father first published The Ohio Repository.

CLAYTON G. HORN

"I know of no other newspaper man in Ohio with greater integrity."

— C. WILLIAM O'NEILL, CHIEF JUSTICE OF THE OHIO SUPREME COURT, SPEAKING AT THE RETIREMENT DINNER FOR CLAYTON HORN IN 1972.

ABOUT

- Born 1906 in Bellevue, Ohio; died 1993 in Canton.
- Visionary journalist, benefactor, humanitarian and community leader.
- Began his journalism career as a sportswriter for The Canton Repository in 1928.
- Worked as managing editor of East Liverpool Review before returning to Canton as editor of The Repository and executive editor of Brush-Moore Newspapers.
- Instrumental in ensuring Interstate 77 and other major highways passed through Canton.
- Was one of the founders of Stark Tech (now Stark State) and was critical in Kent State University's Stark campus locating in Stark County.
- Played a vital role, through The Repository, in attracting the Pro Football Hall of Fame to Canton.

STARK CONNECTION

- Active in Kiwanis, Rotary and National Press Club.
- Served on the boards of Walsh University (then Walsh College) and Kent State University Stark.
- A charter member and a 30-year board member of the Pro Football Hall of Fame.

179

RALPH REGULA

ABOUT

- Born Dec. 3, 1924.
- Elected to Congress 18 straight times, serving a total of 36 years before retiring in 2009; Republican representing Stark County residents and others in the 16th District.
- Considered a political moderate with a reputation for crossing party lines. Known for low-key style.
- Served 1944-46 in the U.S. Navy; private practice lawyer, teacher and school principal.
- Advocated for what would become Stark State College.
- First elected to Congress in 1972 and was in office when President Richard Nixon resigned.
- Served on the powerful House Appropriations Committee.

"You must keep your word in politics. Do your job. Take care of the people and the rest will happen."

- Championed the preservation of what would become Cuyahoga Valley National Park with Democratic U.S. Rep. John Seiberling of Akron Instrumental in creating Ohio & Erie Canalway.

STARK CONNECTION

- Born in Beach City and graduated from Mount Union College in 1948 and the William McKinley School of Law in 1952.
- Lives with wife, Mary, on a farm in Bethlehem Township.

HENRY TIMKEN

"Wherever Wheels and Shafts Turn."

— HENRY TIMKEN'S SLOGAN FOR THE TIMKEN ROLLER BEARING AXLE CO.

ABOUT

- Born Aug. 16, 1831, in Bremen, Germany. Died March 16, 1909, in San Diego, Calif.
- Industrialist who began business as a carriage maker in St. Louis in 1855.
- Obtained a patent for a tapered roller bearing in 1898.
- With his sons, H.H. Timken and William Timken, organized the Timken Roller Bearing Axle Co. in 1899.
- Retired and moved to San Diego, Calif.

STARK CONNECTION

- Timken family moved Timken Roller Bearing Axle Co. to Canton in 1901, because of its proximity to the auto industry in Detroit and Cleveland and to the steel making in Cleveland and Pittsburgh.
- The roller bearing that Henry Timken developed remains the foundation of The Timken Co., which continues to be headquartered in Stark County.
- Inducted in the National Inventors Hall of Fame in Akron in 1998 during a ceremony at E.J. Thomas Hall.

HENRY S. BELDEN

After several years of work with gas street lighting, he saw a stiff mud brick-making machine at the Centennial Exposition in Philadelphia in 1876. It inspired him to make paving and fire brick, which led opening a brick company in Canton.

ABOUT

- One of the founders of the Diebold Fire Brick Co., a predecessor company to Belden Brick.
- Elected mayor of Canton.
- At age 32, moved to the family farm because of a severe throat infection. While there, experimented with coal, shale and clay found at the farm, and created the Belden Burner.
- Earned 13 patents for gasoline vapor street lights and secured contracts for lighting systems in towns and cities across the country.

STARK CONNECTION

- Born here July 4, 1840; died April 21, 1920
- Son of Judge G.W. Belden.
- Served as a lawyer in the Belden & McKinley law offices with William McKinley.

BOB COMMINGS

"I don't care what people say about Paul Brown or Leo Strang or anybody else. I don't think Massillon ever had a better coach than Bob Commings. I can't imagine a better motivator. I knew I could trust him. I was from the southeast side of Massillon. The guys from my end of town respected him."

— FORMER NFL PLAYER TOM HANNON, WHO PLAYED FOR COMMINGS AT MASSILLON.

ABOUT

- Born Dec. 24, 1932, in Youngstown.
- Served in U.S. Army during Korean War.
- Captain and MVP as a guard on Iowa Hawkeyes' 1957 Rose Bowl team.
- Successful football head coach at Struthers, Massillon and GlenOak, compiling 169-66-7 record.
- Went straight from high school coaching at Massillon to be Iowa's head coach.
- In five seasons leading the Hawkeyes from 1974-78, teams produced several surprising wins but just a 17-38 record.
- Died Feb. 20, 1992 in Plain Township.

STARK CONNECTION

- Led Massillon to 43-6-2 record over five seasons, including state poll titles in 1970 and '72. The '70 team outscored opponents 412-29.
- Helped establish GlenOak football program, accumulating 76-44-1 record in 12 seasons as head coach from 1980-91.
- GlenOak tenure included four Federal League titles and, in those days, rare wins against McKinley and Massillon.
- Part of inaugural class for Stark County High School Football Hall of Fame in 2002.
- GlenOak's football field named in his honor in 2007.

THURMAN MUNSON

"Thurman was blue collar. He wasn't afraid to stick his nose in there and mix it up. He'd get bumps and bruises and play with those. His reputation was such that even after he was gone, later-day Yankee players still respected him as a player, and his memory."

— JOE GILHOUSEN, MUNSON'S FRIEND AND TEAMMATE AT LEHMAN AND KENT STATE.

ABOUT

- Born June 7, 1947, in Akron. Died Aug. 2, 1979, in a plane crash while practicing takeoffs and landings at Akron-Canton Airport.
- Played catcher for 11 Major League seasons, all with the New York Yankees, getting selected to seven All-Star Games and winning three Gold Gloves.
- Became the only Yankee to win the Rookie of the Year (1970) and MVP (1976) awards.
- Selected in 1976 as the first team captain of the Yankees since Lou Gehrig in 1939.

- Hit .302 with 17 home runs and 105 RBI during his MVP season, helping the Yankees reach the first of their three straight World Series.
- Helped the Yankees win back-to-back World Series in 1977-78.
- Hit .357 with three homers and 22 RBIs in 30 career postseason games.

STARK CONNECTION

- Starred in baseball, basketball and football at Lehman High School.

DONALD RING MELLETT

"If we have any definable editorial policy it is this — an effort to speak openly and above board on all questions which affect students and their interests."

— DON MELLETT, WHILE EDITOR OF THE DAILY STUDENT AT INDIANA UNIVERSITY.

ABOUT

- Born Sept. 26, 1891, in Elwood, Ind.
- Murdered July 16, 1926, in Canton.
- Son of a newspaper publisher.
- Crusading journalist.
- Came to Canton in 1925.
- Editor and publisher of Canton Daily News.
- Don Mellett Memorial Lecture in Journalism and Don R. Mellett Prize named after him

- Inducted into the Indiana Journalism Hall of Fame in 1969.

STARK CONNECTION

- Crusaded through editorials to clean up a crime-ridden Canton in the mid-1920s, paying for it with his life.
- His journalistic contributions earned the Canton Daily News the Pulitzer Prize, exhibited at McKinley Museum.

EDWARD T. HEALD

"In the new age which Stark faces, the world of the St. Lawrence Seaway, the European Common Market, the atomic age, the missile and the jet airplane, and the fateful struggle between Freedom and Communism, it is well to remind ourselves and the coming generations of the qualities that produced our present greatness, and not lose the spirit of America ..."

— EDWARD T. HEALD, PREFACE TO THE STARK COUNTY STORY, THE AMERICAN WAY OF LIFE.

ABOUT
- Born Sept. 20, 1885, in Portland, Oregon.
- Died June 1, 1967, in Canton.
- Local historian.

STARK CONNECTION
- Author of the six-volume The Stark County Story and biographies of William McKinley.
- Worked for the YMCA in Russia during World War I and later in Canton.
- Helped found the Stark County Historical Society in 1946.

RALPH HAY

"He's the one who had the drive and determination to start a league. They needed a league. Everybody talked about it, but didn't get it done. He did."

— DR. JAMES KING, HAY'S GRANDSON, WHO LIVES IN JACKSON TOWNSHIP.

ABOUT
- Born Jan. 12, 1891, in Canton.
- Died July 29, 1944, in Canton.
- Owned the Canton Bulldogs from 1918-23 when they were one of the top professional football teams in the country.
- Formed the American Professional Football Conference in 1920 (which would become the NFL), with the first organizational meeting taking place in his automobile showroom in downtown Canton.
- His Canton Bulldogs became the first team to win back-to-back NFL titles in 1922 and 1923, when they enjoyed a 23-game streak without a defeat.

STARK CONNECTION
- Graduated from high school in Canton and immediately went to work for a car dealership, quickly excelling as a salesman.
- Formed the Ralph E. Hay Motor Co. in his mid-20s on the corner of Cleveland Avenue and Second Street SW, one of the largest car dealerships in the area, selling Hupmobiles, Jordans and Pierce-Arrows.

FRANK DeVOL

ABOUT

- Born 1911 in West Virginia; died 1999.
- Prolific songwriter and music arranger for television, movies and stage performers for more than seven decades.
- Wrote scores and theme music for more than 50 films, including "Pillow Talk," "The Dirty Dozen," "Guess Who's Coming to Dinner," "Under the Yum Yum Tree," and "Cat Ballou."
- Composed theme music for television shows such as "My Three Sons," "Family Affair," "The Love Boat," and "The Brady Bunch."
- Arranged songs for a multitude of performers, including "Nature Boy" for Nat "King" Cole and "The Happening" for Diana Ross and the Supremes.
- Married to singer Helen O'Connell.
- Acted in such television shows as "Please Don't Eat

"I'm still a name in Canton," Frank DeVol told a Repository reporter in the 1980s, while wryly and modestly commenting on his career. "People know me as one of a group of people from Canton who are considered famous."

the Daisies," "Get Smart," "I Dream of Jeannie," "Gidget," "That Girl," "Bonanza," "Different Strokes," and "Fernwood 2 Nite."

STARK CONNECTION

- Grew up in a house on Sixth Street NW near the stage door of the Palace Theatre, where his father led the pit band.
- Graduated from McKinley High School.
- Returned to Canton often to attend school reunions and help raise funds for charitable causes.

MACY GRAY

"I had all that success really early and I don't think I had a plan to make it last. I just kind of took it for granted and assumed that it would be like that for the rest of my life."

— HUFFINGTON POST INTERVIEW.

ABOUT

- Born Sept. 6, 1967, in Canton as Natalie McIntyre.
- Sold 6 million copies worldwide of her debut album, "On How Life Is."
- Achieved fame following release of her wildly popular single "I Try," a soul-infused pop ballad highlighting her distinctive, raspy voice.
- Won Grammy for best female pop vocal performance for "I Try."
- Has collaborated with Justin Timberlake, Fergie and Natalie Cole.

- In 2009, appeared on "Dancing with the Stars."
- Gray's acting career includes appearances in "Training Day," "The Paperboy" and "Cardboard Boxer."

STARK CONNECTION

- After her fledgling music career stalled in Los Angeles, she returned to Canton before ascending to stardom with her 1999 debut album.
- Returns to Canton to visit family.

MARILYN MANSON

"Marilyn Manson is a criticism of gimmickry, while being itself a gimmick."

— MARILYN MANSON

ABOUT

- Born Jan. 5, 1969, as Brian Hugh Warner in Canton.
- Combined the iconic names of Marilyn Monroe and Charles Manson for his stage name.
- Formed Marilyn Manson and the Spooky Kids while working as an entertainment journalist in Fort Lauderdale, Fla.
- The band later dropped "the Spooky Kids" and had its first mainstream success in the early 1990s.
- Produced hits such as "The Beautiful People," "The Dope Show," "Personal Jesus," and a cover of the Eurythmics' "Sweet Dreams (Are Made of These)"
- Known for on-stage antics and his controversial goth rocker persona.

STARK CONNECTION

- A Canton native.
- Has never played a show in his hometown.

IDA SAXTON McKINLEY

"My wife, be careful, Cortelyou, how you tell her — Oh, be careful."

— REPORTEDLY, PRESIDENT McKINLEY'S WORDS AFTER HE WAS SHOT IN BUFFALO IN 1901.

ABOUT

- Born June 8, 1847; died May 26, 1907.
- From 1868 to 1871, worked in the bank of her father, banker and businessman James Saxton.
- At age 23, she married William McKinley, on Jan. 25, 1871, in First Presbyterian Church in Canton.
- Endured the deaths of two children in the 1870s, Ida and Katie, and suffered from health problems most of her life.
- As wife of McKinley, served as first lady for both the state and the nation.
- Known for knitting slippers for fundraising for various organizations.
- Entombed with her husband and daughters in the McKinley National Memorial.

STARK CONNECTION

- Granddaughter of Repository founder John Saxton.
- Was born and died in Canton, and was educated at Canton Union School.

185

ATLEE POMERENE

ABOUT

- Born Dec. 6, 1863, in Berlin, Holmes County.
- Ohio tax commissioner from 1906-08.
- Ohio lieutenant governor from January to April 1911, when he, a Democrat, resigned after Ohio Legislature elected him to U.S. Senate. After 1913, with passage of 17th Amendment, elected by people in 1916 to serve a fresh six-year term and served as senator until 1923. He lost his bid for re-election in 1922 without the support of the powerful railroad unions and the Anti-Saloon League and made a failed bid for a Senate seat in 1926.
- Played a role in establishing the Federal Tariff Commission and backed the League of Nations.
- Appointed by President Calvin Coolidge to be a special prosecutor in the Teapot Dome

> "He stands against all abuses of political power and favors the restoration of old-time honesty. He stands before us as a man of superior intellect, sound judgment and the moral courage to stand for positive convictions. He has faith in the people and the people have confidence in him."
> — OWEN J. EVANS, STARK COUNTY RESIDENT WHO DELIVERED SPEECH BEFORE OHIO LEGISLATURE'S DEMOCRATIC CAUCUS NOMINATING POMERENE FOR THE U.S. SENATE IN 1911.

scandal.
- Appointed by President Herbert Hoover to be chairman of the Reconstruction Finance Corp.
- Died Nov. 12, 1937, in Cleveland.

STARK CONNECTION

- Practiced law in Canton, serving as Canton City solicitor from 1887 to 1891 and Stark County prosecutor from 1897 to 1900.

MARY N. ORR

"I like acting. I'm a writer because I married a writer and it's nice to be able to do two things."

ABOUT

- Born 1912 in Brooklyn, N.Y.; died Sept. 22, 2006, in Manhattan, N.Y.
- Broadway actress, author, playwright.
- Star on Broadway, 1938-1974.
- Author of screenplays and novels, some with her husband, Reggie Denham, with titles including "Diamond in the Sky" and "Rich Girl, Poor Girl."
- Her short story and radio play, "The Wisdom of Eve," was turned into the movie "All About Eve," which was nominated for 14 Academy

Awards. It won six.
- With her husband, she wrote four plays that opened on Broadway, with the most successful being "Wallflower" in 1944.

STARK CONNECTION

- Moved as a child with her family to Canton, and her family lived on Market Avenue N.
- Attended both McKinley and Lehman high schools.
- Her father, Chester Andrew Orr, was president of Union Metal Manufacturing Co.

HARRY STUHLDREHER

ABOUT

- Born Oct. 14, 1901 in Massillon, died Jan. 26, 1965 in Pittsburgh.
- One of the "Four Horseman" in one of Notre Dame's most storied eras of football.
- Quarterback of a 1924 Fighting Irish team whose other "Horsemen" were Jim Crowley, Elmer Layden and Don Miller.
- The "Horsemen" became larger than life, but none was a big man, and Stuhldreher went 5-foot-7, 150 pounds.
- Stuhldreher's book, "Knute Rockne, Man Builder," was an important source for the film "Knute Rockne, All-American," starring Ronald Reagan as "The Gipper."
- Associated with the "Hail Mary" expression for scoring a dramatic touchdown. Crowley used this story as a staple in many speeches: During a tense game against Georgia Tech, Fighting Irish lineman Noble Kizer suggested a Hail Mary prayer. Shortly thereafter, Stuhldreher threw a touchdown pass on fourth down. After the game, Kizer said, "That Hail Mary is the best play we've got."
- Head football coach at Wisconsin from 1936-50 after an 11-year run at Villanova.
- Best win as a head coach was a 17-7 Wisconsin victory over Massillon legend Paul Brown's No. 1-ranked Ohio State team in 1942.

STARK CONNECTION

- Grew up in Massillon when Rockne played for the pro Massillon Tigers. According to his biography in the College Football Hall of Fame, was invited into a game when he offered to carry Rockne's equipment bag.
- Charter member of the Stark County High School Football Hall of Fame.

"Even as a freshman, Harry had the most promise of the Four Horsemen. He sounded the leader on the field."
— KNUTE ROCKNE.

JUDGE JOHN R. MILLIGAN

ABOUT

- Born April 9, 1928, in East Liverpool and grew up in Lakewood.
- Graduated from Lakewood High School in 1946; College of Wooster in 1949; and University of Michigan Law School in 1952.
- Appointed by President Ronald Reagan in 1982 to be a member of the National Advisory Committee on Juvenile Justice and Delinquency Prevention.
- Served for several years as a visiting judge during his retirement until 2015.
- Won the Ohio State Bar Association's Thomas J. Moyer Award for Judicial Excellence in 2011.

STARK CONNECTION

- Served as Canton City prosecutor from 1954-58 and

"So there was a need of services and facilities that simply weren't there in five counties. We called it a shotgun marriage because it was one of necessity. The small counties needed detention. The bigger counties like ours needed longer term habilitation plans."
— MILLIGAN, IN OCTOBER 2016 IN AN INTERVIEW TALKING ABOUT THE CREATION OF THE MULTI-COUNTY JUVENILE ATTENTION SYSTEM.

as assistant Canton solicitor from 1957-60.
- Appointed to Stark County's Domestic Relations Court, now Family Court, in 1963.
- Played major role in working with judges and county commissioners in Stark, Carroll, Wayne, Tuscarawas and Columbiana counties to create the Multi-County Juvenile Attention System to detain and rehabilitate juvenile offenders. It opened in 1970.
- Elected to the Ohio 5th District Court of Appeals in 1980, before he retired in 1992. Now a resident of North Canton.

WILLIAM E. UMSTATTD

ABOUT

- Born in Bristol, Tenn., in 1894, the son of a department store manager.
- Served in the U.S. Army's ambulance corps during World War I, seeing action in the Marne and the Argonne.
- Learned about Timken Co. while serving in France, where he was impressed by the performance of trucks equipped with Timken bearings and met soldiers from Canton who told him about the company.

STARK CONNECTION

- Hired by Timken in November 1919 as an inspector of finished bearings. Promoted to foreman in the assembly department by the end

"We are going to change the minds of engineers around the world to the point where they use the best bearing instead of just bearings that are better than a friction bearing."

— UMSTATTD ON HIS HOPES THAT ENGINEERS WOULD SEE THE VALUE OF TAPERED ROLLER BEARINGS OVER BALL BEARINGS AND CYLINDRICAL ROLLER BEARINGS.

of 1920.
- Named company president in June 1934 and served 25 years until retiring in 1959.
- Became chairman when he retired and remained in that position until he died on Dec. 2, 1973.
- A driving force behind Canton's bid to become home to the Professional Football Hall of Fame.
- The Umstattd Performing Arts Hall is named for him.

GERHARDT ZIMMERMANN

"For us to preserve the music of the past, we must enable the music of the future."

ABOUT

- Born June 23, 1945, in Van Wert, Ohio.
- Before contracting polio as a boy, Zimmermann wanted to be second baseman for the Cincinnati Reds.
- After joining the orchestra at Bowling Green State University as a trumpet player, he decided to become an orchestra conductor.
- Was the music director of the Raleigh-based North Carolina Symphony from 1982 through 2002.
- Has been on the podium with major symphony orchestras in Cleveland, Chicago, Pittsburgh, Atlanta and Chicago.

- Since 2006, has been director of orchestral activities at the University of Texas in Austin.
- Has homes in Raleigh and Austin with his wife, Sharon, with whom he has two children.

STARK CONNECTION

- Now in his 36th season as musical director for the Canton Symphony Orchestra.
- Has conducted Canton Symphony concerts featuring Bela Fleck, Andre Watts, Yo Yo Ma and Emanuel Ax.

MARION MOTLEY

ABOUT

- Born June 5, 1920, in Leesburg, Ga.
- Died June 27, 1999, in Cleveland.
- Starred with the Browns in the AAFC and NFL for much of his pro football career, playing 99 of his 106 pro games with Cleveland.
- Broke the color barrier in professional football in 1946 when he joined the Browns — one year before Jackie Robinson made his Major League Baseball debut with the Brooklyn Dodgers.
- Rushed for 4,720 career yards and scored 31 TDs, averaging 5.7 yards per carry.
- Helped the Browns win five league champions in six years from 1946-51.
- Averaged 113.3 yards per game on 8.1 yards per carry in playoff games from 1946-49.
- Inducted into the Pro Football Hall of Fame in 1968.

"He looked bigger than anyone else on the field, bigger than any of the linemen. It was hard to find a 240-pound guard (in those days), let alone a fullback that big."

— PRO FOOTBALL HALL OF FAME LINEBACKER DAVE ROBINSON, WHO GREW UP VIEWING MOTLEY AS ONE OF HIS HEROES AND BECAME HIS FRIEND LATER IN LIFE.

STARK CONNECTION

- Moved to Canton from Alabama at age 2 with his family.
- Starred at McKinley High School from 1936-38, first as starting guard as a sophomore before moving to running back his final two years (and averaging 17.2 yards per carry in rushing for 2,178 career yards).
- Helped open Fawcett Stadium in 1938, scoring 17 touchdowns that season, including the "Motley Dribble," in which he went off right tackle for 25 yards, dropped the ball and scooped it back up on a bounce at full speed and ran the remaining 25 yards for the score.

JIM "BISH" HILLIBISH

ABOUT

- Died Sept. 6, 2014, at age 65.
- Worked on newspapers for both Glenwood High School and Kent State University.
- Served in the U.S. Army from 1971 to 1974, as a public affairs specialist in the Armed Forces Staff College in Norfolk, Va., receiving the Joint Meritorious Service Medal from the Joint Chiefs of Staff.
- Worked for The Canton Repository for parts of five decades, writing news stories, feature and entertainment articles, editorials and general interest commentaries, as well as columns on gardening, cooking and computers.
- Held positions at the Repository as photographer, reporter, columnist, entertainment writer, features editor, bureau chief, lifestyle section editor, city editor, editorial writer and Editorial Board member.
- Helped create the newspaper's entertainment section, and, in 1996, designed and launched the award-winning website CantonRep.com.
- Developed and taught an advanced writing course for University of Mount Union and was a frequent speaker to students and civic organizations.
- Received the Distinguished Alumni Award of Kent State University Stark Campus in 2004 and in 2005 was given the Writer of the Year Award from Greater Canton Writers' Guild.

STARK CONNECTION

- Was born in Canton and was influenced by his mother, who taught journalism in high school, then began his career as a child, publishing a neighborhood newspaper on an old press purchased by his dad.
- Developed and promoted the Food For All project through Stark County Hunger Task Force.
- Named a "Most Interesting Person" in Stark County in 2013.

"I just wrote about things I was interested in, and I guess I was interested in a lot of different things."

— JIM HILLIBISH, ABOUT HIS VARIED TOPICS FOR WRITING.

CLYDE SINGER
"I found that every place I go is a painting."

— CLYDE SINGER, ON NEW YORK CITY.

ABOUT

- Born 1908 in Malvern; died 1999 in Youngstown.
- In his 65 years as a working artist, completed more than 3,000 oil and watercolor paintings.
- In 1933, received a scholarship to the Arts Students' League in New York City, where his mentors were "American Scene" painters John Steuart Curry and Thomas Hart Benton.
- In 1940, became the assistant director at the Butler Institute of American Art in Youngstown, where he continued to work until his death.
- Singer's paintings, many of them bustling street scenes, have been exhibited at the Whitney Museum, the Corcoran Gallery, the Chicago Art Institute and the National Academy of Design.

STARK CONNECTION

- In 2008, Singer was the subject of a major posthumous exhibition, "Clyde Singer's America," that was split between the Canton Museum of Art and Butler Institute.
- The exhibition was accompanied by a book "Clyde Singer's America," written by M.J. Albacete, then executive director of the Canton Museum of Art.

GEORGE BELDEN FREASE
"Print only the truth; always be fair."

— TWO OF GEORGE B. FREASE'S FIVE RULES GOVERNING THE PUBLICATION OF A NEWSPAPER.

ABOUT

- Born 1861; died 1928.
- Graduated from high school in Canton, and attended Cincinnati Law School, but became interested in journalism.
- Started at the Repository as a printer and reporter in 1880 at age 19.
- Purchased the Repository from the heirs of Thomas Saxton in 1886.
- Personal friend of President William McKinley, he served as an adviser, publishing McKinley's 1896 campaign newspaper.
- With the assistance of longtime co-owner John C. Dueber, helped a struggling daily Repository grow to one of the most profitable newspapers in Ohio.
- Sold The Canton Repository to Brush-Moore Newspapers not long before his death.

STARK CONNECTION

- Son of Stark County Judge Joseph Frease.
- According to a Repository editorial at his death, he "gave his support quietly but efficiently to worthwhile civic affairs."

190

ESTHER ARCHER

"People like Esther Arthur and Essie Wooten, they set the stage for Chris (Smith) and myself to move forward."

— CANTON CITY COUNCILMAN THOMAS WEST, AT A TRIBUTE TO BLACK POLITICIANS.

ABOUT

- Was the first black woman in Ohio elected to a municipal office in 1948.
- Fought against racism with real estate agent and friend Vera Elliott by purchasing a house in a segregated neighborhood and becoming a licensed real estate agent.
- Was known as a persuasive speaker and community advocate.

STARK CONNECTION

- Served four terms as a Democrat on Canton City Council.
- Was among the first black women hired by the Timken Co.

B. VIRDOT (SAMUEL STONE)

"I am a girl of fourteen. I am writing this because I need clothing. And sometimes we run out of food."

— FROM THE 1933 LETTER TO B. VIRDOT BY HELEN PALM, THE LAST SURVIVING LETTER WRITER, WHO DIED IN 2012 AT 92.

ABOUT

- Refugee from Romania, born an orthodox Jew, who came to the United States early in his teens.
- A Canton businessman who achieved financial successes and suffered through setbacks.
- At Christmas 1933, under the name of B. Virdot, advertised in The Canton Repository to give out small financial gifts to white-collar workers in need.
- In 2010, Stone's Depression-era generosity became the subject of a book, "A Secret Gift," written by his grandson, investigative reporter Ted Gup.
- The "Secret Gift" story subsequently spread throughout the country on network television news, over public radio, and with stories in such publications as the Repository, the New York Times, Wall Street Journal and Smithsonian magazine.
- "A Secret Gift" later was chosen as the highlighted book in the "One Book, One Community" literacy program in Stark County.

STARK CONNECTION

- Owner and operator of a clothing store in Canton.
- Following the publication of "A Secret Gift," the Repository and United Way collaborated to re-create the B. Virdot charity program, raising tens of thousands of dollars for needy families in the Stark County area.

STEPHEN A. PERRY

"Whenever I travel and tell people I'm the executive director of the Pro Football Hall of Fame, they always say what a dream job of a lifetime. And it is."

ABOUT

- Led the Pro Football Hall of Fame's Future 50 development program while he served as the president and executive director from 2006 to 2013.
- Administrator for the U.S. General Services Administration under President George W. Bush from 2001 to 2005.
- Director of Ohio's Department of Administrative Services under Gov. George Voinovich from 1991 to 1993.
- Spent most of his career with the Timken Co., serving as vice president for human resources from 1993 to 1997 and senior vice president from 1997 to 2001.

STARK CONNECTION

- Born in Canton, September 1945.
- Timken High School graduate.

DR. BYRON L. OSBORNE

"This Quaker pastor, educator and author wasted none of his 90 years, and his influence has been spread far and wide ... His life was an affirmation of his faith."

— JUNE 23, 1990, REPOSITORY EDITORIAL ON HIS DEATH.

ABOUT

- Born May 27, 1894, in Greensboro, N.C.
- Died June 20, 1990, at age 96, in North Canton.
- Founded the modern Malone University.
- In 1957, relocated the Cleveland Bible College from Cleveland to Canton, renamed the school Malone College after its founders and rebuilt it as a liberal arts institution.
- Married wife Ruth Malone, daughter of Cleveland Bible College founders Emma and Walter Malone, in 1916.

STARK CONNECTION

- Longtime member and minister of Evangelical Friends Church in Plain Township.
- Worked at Malone as a professor, dean, vice president and president of the college from 1950 to his retirement in 1961.
- After his retirement, returned to preaching. Later became a public speaker and writer.

SHARON LANE

"Born to honor, ever at peace."

— INSCRIPTION ON A MONUMENT HONORING SHARON LANE OUTSIDE AULTMAN HOSPITAL.

ABOUT

- Born July 7, 1943 in Zanesville.
- Died on June 8, 1969, from a neck wound suffered when a 122mm rocket hit her hospital ward in Vietnam; a 12-year-old Vietnamese girl also died, and 27 others were injured.
- Worked at Aultman Hospital before joining the Army Nurse Corps Reserve in 1968.
- Achieved the rank of first lieutenant and worked at the 312th Evacuation Hospital's Vietnamese Ward in Chu Lai, where she treated war-injured and ill Vietnamese civilians as well as Vietnamese POWs.

- Only American servicewoman killed as a direct result of enemy fire in the Vietnam War.
- Posthumously awarded a Purple Heart, Bronze Star, Vietnam Service Medal, National Defense Service Medal and Vietnamese Gallantry Cross.
- Inducted into the Ohio Veterans Hall of Fame.

STARK CONNECTION

- Grew up in North Industry in Stark County.
- Graduate of Canton South High School in 1961.
- Graduated from the Aultman Hospital School of Nursing in 1965.
- Buried at Sunset Hills Cemetery.

JIM THORPE

"You, sir, are the greatest athlete in the world."

— SWEDEN'S KING GUSTAV V, WHOSE NATION HOSTED THE 1912 OLYMPICS.

ABOUT

- Born May 28, 1887, in Lincoln County, Okla.
- Died March 28, 1953 in Lomita, Calif.
- Selected the Greatest Athlete of the 20th Century in a 1999 ABC poll, beating out the likes of Babe Ruth, Muhammad Ali, Jesse Owens and Michael Jordan.
- Won gold medals in the 1912 Olympics in the pentathlon and decathlon.
- Starred in track, baseball, lacrosse, ballroom dancing and football at the Carlisle Indian Industrial School in Pennsylvania, leading the football program to a famous 27-6 win over a powerful Army football team.
- Played both pro football and baseball.

STARK CONNECTION

- Starting in 1915, became a star of the powerful Canton Bulldogs pro football teams, leading the team to Ohio League championships from 1917-19.
- Named president of the American Professional Football Association (which would become the NFL) when it was formed in Canton in 1920.
- Played the 1920 season with the Canton Bulldogs, then spent 1921-25 playing elsewhere before returning in 1926 for a final season in Canton.

JOHN SAXTON

ABOUT

- Born Sept. 28, 1792; died April 16, 1871.
- Served in the Army during War of 1812 and learned printing at the Huntingdon (Pa.) Gazette.
- Married Margaret Laird, and came to Canton in 1814, founding The Ohio Repository on March 30, 1815.
- Published a few hundred of his four-page paper weekly on a hand press, working late into the night by candle light.
- Preferred to be called "printer," instead of "editor" or "publisher."
- Saxton published his first major story in his newspaper on Aug. 24, 1815, about Napoleon's defeat at Waterloo in June, using information published New York and Philadelphia papers based on dispatches from Boston.

- Handed over daily publication of the Repository to his son, Thomas, but continued to come to the newspaper's office to set type until his death at age 79.

STARK CONNECTION

- During his time in Canton, Saxton served as a commercial printer, land agent, postmaster and county treasurer.
- As a member of a Canton Presbyterian church, Saxton, said his obituary, "was a Christian all over, in daily work, in heart and in purse."
- He and his wife had eight children — seven sons — who contributed to the Canton community, including James Saxton, influential in banking, and Thomas Saxton, who took over from his father the publication of the Repository.

"We have never sought to make our paper anything but a truthful record of the passing tidings of the times. We have endeavored to cast our influence on the side of right."

— FROM AN EDITORIAL JOHN SAXTON WROTE IN 1864, AT THE BEGINNING OF HIS 50TH YEAR OF PUBLICATION OF THE OHIO REPOSITORY.

PAUL BROWN

"Paul Brown integrated pro football without uttering a single word about integration. He just went out, signed a bunch of great black athletes and started kicking butt."

— CLEVELAND BROWNS HALL OF FAMER JIM BROWN.

ABOUT

- Born Sept. 7, 1908, in Norwalk. Died Aug. 5, 1991, in Cincinnati.
- Lost just 10 games in 11 seasons as a high school coach. At Massillon, from 1932-40, finished with a record of 80-8-2 and four national titles.
- Led Ohio State to its first national championship in 1942.
- Won four All-American Football Conference titles and three NFL titles with the Cleveland Browns, where he was the head coach from 1946-1962.
- Co-founded the Cincinnati Bengals in 1968 and coached the team from 1968-75.

STARK CONNECTION

- Moved to Massillon at 9 years old and graduated from Washington High School in 1925.
- Went 15-3 as the Tigers' starting quarterback in 1923-24.
- Buried at Rose Hill Cemetery in Massillon.

WALTER WELLMAN

"My faith is strong that having demonstrated the practicability of air travel man will go on till he has developed flight into a state of perfection and usefulness not even indicated by the apparatus of today."

— WALTER WELLMAN, WRITING IN 1911 IN THE NEW YORK TIMES SUNDAY MAGAZINE.

ABOUT

- Born Nov. 3, 1858 in Mentor; died Jan. 31, 1934, in New York City.
- Journalist, explorer, adventurer and aeronaut.
- Established a weekly newspaper in Nebraska at 14, then at 21 established the Cincinnati Evening Post.
- Was political and Washington, D.C., correspondent for the Chicago Herald and Record-Herald.
- Cruising in the Bahamas, Wellman and historians attempted to pinpoint the spot at which Christopher Columbus landed in 1492, erecting a monument in San Salvador.
- Led five unsuccessful attempts to reach the North Pole, two by surface expeditions and three by air (dirigible balloons), paving the way for polar exploration by air.
- Retired in New York City and wrote for magazines and books.

STARK CONNECTION

- Married Laura McCann of Canton on Christmas Eve in 1879.
- Was a printer, reporter and city editor at the Repository from 1878-1880.

ANNA McKINLEY

"She was the first member of her family to relocate to Canton. Shortly after her parents, brothers William and Abner, and sister Helen followed."

— FROM A POSTING ON PINTEREST BY WM. McKINLEY PRESIDENTIAL LIBRARY & MUSEUM.

ABOUT

- Born 1832 in Niles; died July 29, 1890, in Canton.
- Daughter of William McKinley Sr. and Nancy Campbell McKinley.
- Sister of President William McKinley.
- Began her teaching career with her sister, Helen, in Cynthiana, Ky.
- Sunday school teacher in the Methodist church, and she also was active in the church's missionary work.

STARK CONNECTION

- Beloved educator and principal in Canton City Schools.
- McKinley High School named after her, not for her more famous brother, William.

STANLEY C. EWING

ABOUT

- Born March 24, 1921, in Wooster; died April 26, 2011.
- Graduated from Lehman High School in 1938; attended Miami University in Oxford.
- Joined the Navy on Nov. 10, 1942, was awarded a Bronze Star.
- Graduated from the Cleveland School of Merchandising and Management in 1948, then joined his father as a Chevrolet dealer.
- Member of the National Automobile Dealers' Association, The Ohio Automobile Dealers' Association, and was named president of the Stark County Automobile Dealers' Association.

STARK CONNECTION

- Lifetime member of the Automotive Hall of Fame.
- Served the community as past president of the Greater Canton Chamber of Commerce, receiving the Chamber's Award of Appreciation in 1991 for outstanding service to the community.
- Member of the Canton Rotary Club for more than 60 years.
- Recognized as a Paul Harris Fellow.
- Founding member of the Glenwood High School Booster Club.
- 70-year member of Church of the Savior United Methodist.
- Instrumental in bringing the Canton Indians' minor league 'AA' baseball team to Canton.
- In 1993, he was inducted into the Senior Olympics Hall of Fame and the Stark County Baseball Hall of Fame.
- Donated the Stan and Dee Ewing Varsity Center in 1993 to Malone College in honor of Dee.
- Member of the Ancient Accepted Order Scottish Rite, of Tadmor Temple and the Canton Shrine Club.

"... He was humble, intelligent and kind. He told me there is 'no right way to do a wrong thing' and many other maxims that have guided my life."

— BARB EWING COCKROFT

JAMES "ED" WITMER

"The good operation and reputation of SMHA today started with Ed; he set the high standards."

— STARK METROPOLITAN HOUSING AUTHORITY BOARD MEMBER RUTHE FREED TOLD THE CANTON REPOSITORY IN 1998 FOR A STORY ABOUT WITMER'S DEATH.

ABOUT

- Born July 30, 1912, in Canton.
- Died Aug. 5, 1998, in Canton.
- Owner and publisher of Presto Press Printers and Publishers.

STARK CONNECTION

- Served two terms in Ohio House in 1940s.
- State senator from 1957 to 1964.
- Lost congressional race to Frank T. Bow in 1962.
- Five terms as secretary of Canton Federation of Labor.
- Active in many community and civic organizations.
- Served on committees that named Alliance "Carnation City" and Louisville "Constitution Town."
- Director of Stark County Metropolitan Housing Authority from 1970 to 1982.
- Witmer Arms apartments in Massillon are named for him.

REBECCA STALLMAN

"I believe that each person is unique and has great personal worth no matter how severe the handicaps."

ABOUT

- Born in 1945 in Canton.
- A dedicated mentor to the mentally and physically disabled.
- Chosen in 2001 as Professional of the Year by Arc of Stark County.

STARK CONNECTION

- Served the Stark County Board of Mental Retardation and Developmental Disabilities for four decades.
- Primarily worked at Southgate School.
- Twice named Teacher of the Year.

STUART WILKINS

"He was just a tough, tough kid. After high school, in the Big Ten, he was considerably smaller than most of the guys he blocked. But he was smarter than everybody else. He'd face a guy 50 pounds bigger. He wouldn't hurt them, but he'd win, almost every time."

— FORMER McKINLEY AND MICHIGAN FOOTBALL STAR DICK KEMPTHORN, IN 2008 ABOUT HIS FORMER HIGH SCHOOL OPPONENT AND COLLEGE TEAMMATE

ABOUT

- Born Feb. 25, 1928, in Canton.
- Died March 29, 2011 in Canton.
- Started all four years as a guard on the University of Michigan football team from 1945-48, winning national titles in 1947 and 1948.
- Graduated from University of Michigan Law School and was a senior partner and one of the founding members of the Krugliak, Wilkins, Griffiths & Dougherty law firm.

STARK CONNECTION

- Earned All-Ohio honors in football in 1944 at Lincoln High School, starring as an offensive tackle and linebacker.
- Charter member of the steering committee appointed to bring the Pro Football Hall of Fame to Canton.
- Founding member of the Hall of Fame's Board of Trustees, serving on it for 45 years, including as Secretary from 1962-84 and Chairman from 1985-97.
- Enshrined into the Stark County High School Football Hall of Fame in 2008.

197

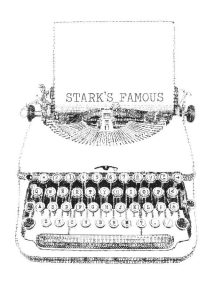